IDK GOD

Conversations with God
in the chaos of becoming someone new.

Becki Jean Graves

D1518182

ISBN: 9798869566386

This book is for you.

Where you are, right now.

Not who you hope to be.

Or who you've been.

But you, right now.

Note to the Reader

Within these pages, you'll find a collection of words from my ever-evolving life captured in real time.

When I found the ground was moving underneath me, I started talking and writing. From working in ministry to leaving ministry, deconstruction and reconstruction, marriage, friendship, parenthood, and the ordinary in between....I have a feeling there may be something in here that will help you feel seen and a little less lonely.

The flow of this book, much like life's lessons, is not bound by chronological order. It's here to encourage us to embrace the process and little moments of growth instead of glorifying the bookends. As you read, I encourage you to jump around with me, accept the intentional disorder and the reflections that each excerpt inspires within you.

You'll find entries titled About Me Right Now throughout this book. I have used this prompt to help me process how I am doing and what I'm carrying in real time. I still do. Feel free to borrow it if you so choose.

I sure hope reading this feels like you're sitting down with a friend, receiving a warm hug, or hearing a hearty "Me too!" I still am unsure of a lot. But I know I found God again when I started talking and writing.

It is my prayer you will too.

Contents

UNLEARNING

The intentional letting go of what we have learned and the openness to explore our own personal truths and be liberated from our past conditionings.

NOTHING IS WASTED

The phrase "nothing is wasted" is one that's been around my whole life.

Like many words and phrases, this one takes on another meaning as I get older and experience more life.

Lately, this phrase has taken on a combative role.

The voices in my head are fine-tuned to failure.

If I don't nail it the first time (regardless of experience), I'm a failure.

Yet as I grow, the opposite is true.

Failure isn't the initial miss.

Failure is experienced when we don't do anything with what we've missed.

Failure doesn't have a timeline, because it's never too late to switch-up your mindset.

So, what does a growth mindset look like? Nothing is wasted. Nothing.

Anything we encounter in our days is an opportunity to learn. An artist I love says, "Humility is embracing our humanness".

A life full of waste can be redeemed.

Maybe it's not a waste at all.

We cannot grow into who we are created to be without being wrong and learning from it.

What if we weren't so stinking hard on ourselves when we miss? How can we know something if we don't experience it?

My point? Failure lies have a specific tone and underlying message: Condemning. Feeling hopeless and helpless. Fear, isolation, and shame. The message is almost always a hit at your identity.

So, your head is filled with "I'll never" or "it's pointless" or "I can't".

It forces you to live a fearful, tight gripped life in the illusion of control. It teaches you that failure is avoidable and must never happen.

In reality, failure is opportunity.

Failure's voice invites you to see you're not perfect, nor are you supposed to be. It invites you to a deeper, fuller life.

How can we know how to comfort, interact, and heal if we are so hard on ourselves for needing those things in the first place?

It breeds beautiful traits; empathy and forgiveness for self and others to name a few.

So, let's take off the lens of failure and replace it with a growth mindset.

You gossiped about a friend and she found out.

Own it. Apologize. Ask for forgiveness.

You didn't get something right the first or millionth time. Grace, friend.

Grace and more grace.

You and your significant other fight more than others. So what????? What are you learning from it?

You bombed the first time you were trusted to teach or coach a group of people. Well, you've never done it before. So, you have room to grow.

Don't let the fear of failure keep you from growing. From the start.

Everyone fails.

Some people cover it and try desperately to make you believe they can never miss. But remember, everyone does.

EVERYONE will and has failed.

The question doesn't change: how did you grow from it?

Nothing is wasted. Even for you, friend.

JOY AND PAIN

We were created to hold joy and pain in both hands.

Often, I find myself overwhelmed and tending to the pain more. Pain manifests worry and guilt about the good parts of my life.

Researcher Brene Brown says joy is one of the most vulnerable emotions, and I think she's right. It's easier to be a cynic, to focus only on what's wrong. Forgoing all hope and refusing to believe things will ever get better.

That's a numb state of pain we place ourselves in—some of the ways we got to that place are outside of our control—but the place is ours to hold.

Throw in anxiety, worry, and depression—it's darker there.

I'm inviting us to a more empowering narrative.

I think pain is allowed because the redemption that comes from it is hard and holy. Pain is given because it helps us become more human and face our own frailty.

Sometimes we think joy is on the other side of pain, but maybe it's meant to co-exist with it.

Maybe we get to hold both and let ourselves feel both.

Even if your joy is as simple as the sun rising and setting each day —that's enough.

Pain is inevitable in our narrative as humans—so what do we do with it?

I'm not attempting to breeze over pain, but rather give movement to it.

It doesn't have to be as dark and lonely.

As vulnerable and debilitating as it can be, it's also an invitation to connect. Letting others in, to see you and care for you.

Sometimes we think joy is on the other side of pain, but maybe it's meant to co-exist with it.

Some may fail, sure, but that's the risk you're willing to take for those that will not.

In my own anxiety journey, this one is complex for me.

I like to avoid my pain by running to others and serving them.

However, in serving them, I crave the love I've given.

Then get angry and isolated when the love I give isn't returned to me exactly as I gave it. However, how I come back to the center and remember my truth is by isolating myself in a way. So, that's a hot mess to try and figure out.

In my pain, I need to share with someone. But I also need to center on truth for myself.

Joy comes in a grittier form in that space.

It's not immediate happiness, maybe more like peace for the moment.

Every time I share or focus on truth, the load gets lighter.

I talk to God and give Him the laundry list of why I'm worried, afraid, angry, nervous, insecure... I did that this morning in fact, and it helped.

But it didn't take it away totally---I'm left in the space I mentioned earlier.

Holding a day full of joy and people with my anxious thoughts about if I'm loved/who I am/will the world be okay...

I hold both at this moment.

We were created with far more capacity than we realize. The capacity widens as we find our Source and Truth.

The strength to hold both is the result of finding the Truth. God is mine.

So, here's to a Friday filled with joy and the hard stuff. You can do it.

Movement in the hard, stillness in the good.

He holds all things, every child and mountain.

The devastating and the magic.

The earth and all its life.

If He can hold it, and I'm created in His image...with His strength, I can hold both too.

DISCONTENTMENT

It's easy to grow discontentment.

The good that others post about helps me believe I could never have that same good. I often forget how much work happened pre-good thing.

I often throw my hands up to God, telling him I've shown up in this season long enough. I've been obedient and honest.

I want the check mark that ends the season of waiting and hardship.

I want a fresh start.

It's sexier.

The good thing, the accomplishment—that brings me worth and purpose.

The stuff I'm asked to do here is just hard.

To show up on the daily and face the people and emotions of the hard—it gets old fast. You see the ugly parts of you that show up when all the attention and accolades leave, and you're left with your discontentment.

Comparison causes us to look at the dusty parts of our lives and quickly proclaim them unworthy.

Comparison says that someone's marriage, job, followers, and opportunity are better than the life given to you right now.

Our houses and families fade into hindsight, and we focus on what new décor is needed, and what flashy thing we need more.

We scroll to suppress and grab more reasons to be discontent—even if we are not fully aware of it.

I'm in a season where I'm being asked to focus on my marriage. How does that bring you glory, God?

I'll tell you how---it's taking all I got.

And that's not because it's hard to love a spouse, though sometimes that's the case.

It's because through loving and showing up for MY spouse, so many lies bubble up to the surface.

Not just bubble, they breach and jump out of the water and splash, humpback whale style.

So, that makes the comparison piece worse at times.

I compare myself as a wife, a lover, and a companion.

To the girl in the magazine, and to my couple friends who have been married for years.

Because I'm working through so much on the daily, discontentment and apathy rear their ugly head on the regular.

"I'm too tired.".

"I'm over it.".

"You don't deserve my kindness or hard work." Just a few thoughts in my head.

Yikes.

But I know you've thought the same.

So, how do we move from discontentment and comparison to a healthy area? One that cultivates contentment and firm footing in where you are.

If I had an easy answer or a quick how-to, I'd tell you.

Unfortunately, in my experience, it requires honesty with yourself and with God. If God isn't your jam, then maybe with someone you trust.

Speaking out discontent, comparison statements that we write and read on the daily...this loosens their claws on our heart and mind.

Call out that crap for what it is.

'Cause I firmly believe we are guided through the seasons of our life. Every season; a purpose.

That's my most recent and tried and true weapon against discontent.

WORRY AND OTHER THINGS

It feels as if we take any steps forward towards hope, it is always met with 10 steps back. Or maybe 10 reasons why hope is futile and naïve.

Choose fear, choose to worry, choose control—even if it's a lie.

At least you'll have something to hold.

It's interesting to me how much worry feels easier than hope. Wild how much fear can become a companion instead of peace. Sometimes if I allow myself to receive peace, I feel guilt.

"I shouldn't need it.", I think.

"Well good, you can't have it.", my fear responds.

But I'm admitting now I need the deep well of hope more than ever.

With ice caps melting, our current political climate, entering into the third round in trying to conceive, and our lead pastor facing a battle with cancer.

On top of that, I worry I cannot give my husband the happiness he needs from me to feel centered.

The spiritual practice of presence is the antidote to anxiety.

I worry I won't get the experience of old age but am also afraid of getting older.

Growing up means facing the myth of control.

It means fighting for your Truth when there are a billion reasons not to.

The only true magical solution is one that is learned with time.

Presence.

Here. Now.

Yes, tomorrow is coming, but it is not here yet. Yes, yesterday has gone, and we cannot get it back. What we do have is right now.

Even now, typing these words...I have won.

How have I won? I refuse to live a life in fear because of the "what ifs" that plague my thoughts.

Sometimes it feels as though I'm fighting my entire body to choose hope, but I must in order to see the gifts around me.

I have the tools to fight around me.

Another week into the unknown, yet I do know I can hold both hope and worry. I can feel worry and remember hope.

The spiritual practice of presence is the antidote to anxiety. If my worry-filled future is coming tomorrow, yet I choose to sit down and laugh with my husband, I have won.

I can be hopeful and grateful that God carries my worry.

And I'm not alone.

That's the other antidote to anxiety—I'm only as alone as I choose to believe I am.

"There are a million reasons to trust You"...even when I don't feel them. I can still choose You.

OOPS I DID IT AGAIN

It happened again.

I read a status, liked a post, and listened to a friend or preacher affirm my opinion, and my ego grew.

My mind became more convinced.

My passion and voice grabbed hold of control.

Weapons drawn, I had someone else who agreed with me on my stance.

We do it all the time.

The rise of ego and inflating of self.

Our biases get confirmed by the like-mindedness around us.

One day, we cannot believe Susan from daycare doesn't go to church.

We cannot believe Grandma would vote for that politician.

We cannot believe our neighbor could love God and not be in church.

We simply cannot believe humans who do _____ , who believe _____, who vote _____ could follow the same God as us.

I was listening to a message at church and was struck by how often this happens with the bible and our approach to it.

I don't often go into scripture trying to soothe or ease my pain.

I go into it trying to prove a point or find that verse that validates mine or the motives of others. It's not often I open up my Bible to be reminded of who Jesus is.

It's not often I come with the right motive—I'm embarrassed to say that.

Yet as I look at the guy whose words are in red, I see what we so often fail at:

He sees the other.

Specifically, the other who is considered an outcast, too far gone, a sinner, a whore, and a robber.

Those who expected to be celebrated by him found themselves being questioned with every encounter.

Those who wanted prestige and a higher pedestal—they missed his message completely.

In fact, it made them rage.

I just think we have it so backward. I think all of us do.

This is the danger of being around people who look, think, and act like you.

Your self-awareness and ability to see and appreciate differences are dimmed as the burning flame of being "right" scorches the other.

Since when did being "right' get anyone anything?

Being "right" about something feeds my own biases about the people who think differently than me.

It's toxic to unity. It really is.

It's too much pressure on someone to always be right and live right and eat right and be right.

When Jesus encountered people in the Bible, he saw them first. He took time to see and understand.

Sometimes he corrected, other times He validated.

But what did the Pharisees do?

Scoffed, questioned, tricked, and used insider law and language that excluded people from life in all senses of the word.

So I ask myself, "In my interactions and conversations—am I a Pharisee or an outcast?" Which heart posture am I taking?

Is it one that includes, no matter what?

Is it one that sees and listens to a life that is different from mine?

I can't say I get it right, even part of the time.

I know I am both Pharisee and outcast, often in the same sentence. But I do know which posture I'd like to take over being right.

Being right gains momentary pleasure or status, but it's an illusion.

We can take small steps to remedy our worship of "being right" by simply admitting we don't know.

By taking someone to coffee who is hard to love (including yourself).

By seeking to understand a view outside your political party.

You can talk about scripture without trying to prove a point.

You can give your grandma some grace because just like you, she has a choice.

You can ask your neighbor how he connects with God instead of judging him for not going to a building like you.

There's just so much we miss because we are obsessed with being better and right.

Maybe, just maybe, there's a richer life out there filled with opinions that make you sweat and heated discussions ending in dinner together.

Don't miss it, friends. We belong to each other.

THE INSTAGRAM MOM & OTHER INSECURITIES

I think I'm a good mom, but I definitely don't think I'm the best. What defines the best, you ask?

Oh you know, the moms you see on Instagram with their perfect hair and outfits. Their leggings are name brand and messy buns, perfected.

There's no hanging tummy pouch from their c-section like I have.

Their kids are their minis--perfectly polished. Not a runny nose to be found.

Their "mess" is basically my version of clean.

Their postpartum bodies have bounced back.

They give advice on meals, breastfeeding, tantrums, and raising emotionally intelligent children. These moms are so in love with their children and it makes me INSECURE.

My goal is never to shame this.

More power to ya. I celebrate you if you are this mom. I'm jealous of you!

I'll admit that.

As a mom, I feel I have only insecure areas. Typing that makes me laugh.

I love my daughter so much.

I love being away from her, too.

I struggle to keep my sanity when I work, then come home for a few hours with just her before bed.

I also have amazing days when we're home all day and my voice is gentle and patient and I do all the age-appropriate sensory activities.

I have plastic and natural toys.

TV is always on.

I have routines that I idolize and that I let go of if we're all tired. We eat mac and cheese and fruit bars *a lot*.

Perhaps this "Instagram mom" I compare myself to compares herself to me.

In fact, I know she does because that's the way it works.

Someone always has something you don't have, someone is always doing it better. It's a losing battle.

Instagram just makes it seem unattainable.

Or maybe our desire to appear polished and perfect, with carefully selected insecure "areas" that we're vulnerable about is the dang issue.

What the heck do you do about it?

Let's start with defining our "best" or "good" when we talk about ourselves as parents.

Why is this insta-mom I follow "best"?

For starters, she's patient. She really seems like it's easy and natural for her to do all the things that go into being a mom.

She's also stunning and her day 7 hair is still silky and shiny.

The sacrifice is seemingly wired within her.

I know that's a load of crap.

No one loves sacrifice...but now I've tapped into an insecurity of mine.

I've *always* wanted to be considered gentle and patient and sacrificial.

My wiring doesn't allow that much.

So it's not natural for me to practice patience, turn off the screens and engage in developmental play, etc.

I get angrier than I care to admit when, God forbid, my daughter doesn't listen.

I really love working outside the home..

So, I've shared my idea of "best" and why it hits my sore spots. What is yours?

Maybe identifying this will help us see it's not actually that insta-mom that needs my attention, it's me.

IT'S ME, HI, I'M THE PROBLEM IT'S ME (Thanks, Taylor).

It's about worth.

It's about knowing there is more than one way to be a parent and raise a kid(s).

It's less of the easy judging and more of doing the inner work to get content with what you have and who you are.

It's supposed to look different. That's the gift.

ABOUT ME RIGHT NOW

I adjusted my "about me" bio on Facebook.

It was hard to find words, and I'm a little thrown off by that, so I just plopped a quote in there that captures my heart...kinda.

Maybe it captures who I want to be.

My about me right now would probably go something like this:

I stand for a lot, and I stand for the space needed to figure out what to stand for.

I'm in a season of total faith destruction and have been for a couple of years now.

I do love people, but now am learning how to love them healthily —not just to please or look good, or be called good.

There are times I feel boxed in and I react by getting angry and mean.

I'm in a season of waiting. Though it's clear I'm supposed to focus on my marriage and write, that doesn't feel like enough.

I want to do something meaningful, so I'm basically saying to God my "right now" isn't enough to be "meaningful", whatever the heck that means.

I'm over closed-hearted doctrines and fear-based mission work, so I desire to rethink and reintroduce God to myself and others.

I hate being misunderstood.

I desperately want to build up other women who are doing what I dream of doing, but it's so hard. She always feels like the cool girl who has the life I want—which steals me from my current reality, which is so important to be present in.

Simple truths and practices are saving my faith. Journaling, practicing presence, and contentment. Getting real honest with God. I felt no condemnation from Him, though some parts of my upbringing would have me believe otherwise.

I miss being joyful. Last night I laughed at myself really hard with my husband. I love when we do that.

Every time I write, I fight anxiety. Tense shoulders raised heartbeat, neck strain...

Sometimes it makes me question whether or not writing through is worth that.

Usually, anxiety comes around when I have something to learn, or when I'm pushing up against something good and meaningful.

I bite my nails down out of boredom or anxiousness.

I'm getting comfy wearing only mascara. It's my symbol to myself I have nothing to prove.

I'm not good at unmotivated serving—I'm learning how much I need affirmation when I sacrifice for others. I choose to help my Joel with something he loves and don't get anything in return...well, I don't want to serve anymore and I think he will never be able to love or serve me as I do him.

GROSS.

This is my current "about me" edition. It's where I am.

I'm learning and growing.

I'm still feisty and strong.

I still have a soft heart.

I still believe in myself and my God.

But, it's complicated. And I'm letting it be so.

Nothing to prove, nothing to lose.

'TWAS THE NIGHT BEFORE THERAPY

I start therapy tomorrow.

What if it all comes crashing down?

What if I've been pretending when I thought I was living authentically?

What if I hate my spouse or God or my parents?

"What if you built ALL of those things on a firm foundation? Waves came, winds blew... You will feel the waves but trust this foundation. Of Me. Of your husband. This is a chance to breathe and heal. This is of Me. I am glorified. It's a good yes".

Nothing on the outside has changed, but my inner world has been released.

I am now 4 months post my first therapy session. Four months past this initial entry.

It's difficult to find words that encompass that journey and who I am on the other side. Nothing on the outside has changed, but my inner world has been released.

I have learned how to hold space for my feelings, not frantically try to name or reason them away. I've learned my body is a vessel. Scripture says our bodies are temples...that's been used and abused in a lot of ways.

But I'm finding just how often the Spirit communicates with our bodies via our gut, shoulders, jaw, and pursed lips.

That in itself is a journey growing up as a woman in the Christian faith.

You mean my body isn't just for the satisfaction of man and for creating life?! Imagine that.

The sarcasm aside, therapy is deeply good. It's hard inner work that spills into your outer world. It's disorienting at first.

Then you settle into the chaos.

Then you find the good spots, the healthy patterns, and you see a more holistic life.

Then you fight to keep it by valuing yourself, your relationships, and your work.

Two paragraphs and the words still don't cover it. Perhaps that is the way it's supposed to be.

More meaningful to be alive than to find the words for it.

FOR THOSE OUTSIDE THE CHURCH PART I

This is fresh.

Coming at you from the middle of a reconstruction of faith after immense deconstruction and pain.

It's a weird place to be, having a place I once belonged and no longer do.

It's weird to be known than not known at all...or known for different things. It's weird to drop my kid off in a nursery and cry through worship.

I miss worship, a lot.

And I don't let myself be sad that part is over.

We went to church today for the third time in a year. All day I've just been weepy.

It all feels so tender.

Opening yourself back up to Jesus, Christianity, and the church...it's a lot.

You could call me a hypocrite because I try to equip students to go throw their lives and work into the church.

"It's worth it!", I say.

"It's the hardest work you'll ever do, and it's worth it.".

But me? My family and our experience? Hard. Complicated.

I gave a talk on church hurt recently.

A student asked me what I would tell my younger self going into ministry...what a question.

Without hesitation, I would tell my younger self to do it. I wouldn't change a thing...that's what makes it hard!

I wish I could be wiser, but I've only grown wise from making a lot of mistakes and hurting a lot of people and thinking I knew everything and I didn't.

So, after all that, here we are. I'm asking myself the same question. Is it worth it to open myself back up to church?

Today it was.

I'll let you know if that stays. I hope it does.

FOR THOSE OUTSIDE THE CHURCH PART II

If you're in this place, it's an odd one to be in....but you're not alone.

Part one of this was long social post I wrote after attending church with my family.

I wept through worship. I let myself feel the devastation of our loss, the anger of having to find a "new" place. I let myself feel grateful for a church founded and run by people I know and trust. It was a safe haven for me/my family to try again.

This post got a lot of attention.

Some from our past church.

A lot more from people who found themselves in the same spot. The circumstances were different, but the feeling bonded us.

It also solidified something within me.

How much I need to keep sharing about our journey post-ministry.

How costly it is to leave a church body...but how freeing it is, too.

How the body of Christ extends so far beyond the church walls and ministry leaders...those extensions, the body parts that are not "public"... show up like Christ in real and tangible ways. They help us heal.

They help us face our own failure.

They help us know it's not forever.

So, I'm committed to being that part of the Body of Christ.

The parts that talk about the grief and loss that comes with church dynamics and failings because it helps others not feel so alone.

That's the work that matters to me.

If you're reading this, and you find yourself in a similar spot...I just want to hug you through the pages.

What happened is valid.

It's real.

It is not forever.

It is not simply "church hurt".

It's a hard part of your story.

It's shaped your faith, now.

It's helped you become softer, knowing the cost of un-belonging to a church body and vision and mission.

You're not alone.

And I hope you won't give up.

But It's okay if you need to right now.

I promise, as you heal, the light comes back. You feel warmth, not just from the tears staining your cheeks...but from a smile and a peaceful heart.

God is with you.

God loves the church, the whole crazy, rowdy, bunch. Deeply.

May you rest in that.

QUARANTINE LESSONS

A sudden gift of slow.

Where time doesn't matter, the normal connection is frayed, and we're left with anxiety and boredom.

Oh, how we worship our time and our schedules.

A routine that boxes up this inner restlessness we all feel deep in our insides.

It asks:

Am I truly living?

Am I doing enough?

Am I loved?

Do I belong?

How can we exist in general? What is life?

Am I using my time well?

Those questions loom, black holes in our hearts and mind.

So we create structure around them. Routine. Helping us feel more in control.

Do I worship God in this self-made structure?

Is routine and fast-paced-achievement-driven success the throne God sits on? Do I worship this god?

Because it can only go so far, it can only fill us so much.

Even if our cup is overflowing, it remains shallow and hollow.

Like eating pizza! Hungry again in an hour.

I'm asking myself, "Who is the God of my life"?

Quarantine has forced this upon me.

Books and the time on my hands have me reflecting on this question.

Because without my regular routines, without the ability to do normal work...I'm left with mostly a hum of anxiety and restlessness.

Yes, God is here.

But that isn't the thought or foundation I'm finding or resting in.

Behind the mists of society, my faux spirituality and belief systems, these are my foundations:

I am only useful to God if I do something.

God has allotted time for rest, but I better get it right because if I do too much I'm lazy but if I don't do enough He'll cast me out

A free and open schedule means I am not fully living my "purpose"

I need to be achieving something else in my career and marriage. I need to be "on track" with everyone else—whatever that means.

I need to be productive and creative, make it count!

These all surfaced quicker than I would've liked.

I wish I could have more spiritual answers.

I don't see much Jesus in these foundations, which explains a lot of the anxiety I feel.

I leave with this thought:

Would God still love and choose me if I couldn't do one thing for him?

Would He still sacrifice his life if we lived in quarantine forever?

Only home. Social distancing. Just us.

Would we still be chosen for Love?

I know the answer is yes. 10,000,000 times over.

But do I believe it?

Working on that.

A LETTER FOR THE FUTURE I THOUGHT WAS MINE

Release is a funny thing.

The dreams I built inside of a building still grip me.

The approval and neglect of a man is difficult lay down.

It's shaped my future here. It's hard when those dreams are rerouted and peeled back again and again. It's easy to not feel believed in, or enough in every sense of the word.

When your job is mixed with your faith, it creates a terribly sensitive, boundary-less life.

Every single event, thought, and conversation is connected. This intermixing brings passion and goodness to what I do. It also brings devastation.

Humans are leaned on more than God.

When your job is mixed with your faith, it creates a terribly sensitive, boundary-less life.

When they hurt me, that must mean God has hurt me. It's not true, but the feelings are strong.

Every change leaves me asking, "Can I go on? Can I still be who I am here?"

So, what if you're asked to let it go?

Let go of what you thought the future would be, and sign up for something unknown. Something that requires you, authentically.

Something that requires the release of control, over and over again. Not the things you can do, but WHO YOU ARE.

Slowly, I'm unclenching my white-knuckle grip on "what could/ should be" and opening my hands.

Open hands, open heart.

There's more room for the new to occupy my heart when the old is surrendered. And about the old...it's not necessarily meant to be released, but built upon.

I have not wasted the last 7 years of my life.

So, until I finally step outside into freedom of the new, I wait.

I lead.

I struggle.

I release my emotions.

My call to lead the church is great.

I could not have known without falling in love with it first.

But more importantly, I serve.

I trust that God is true and honest, deeply.

My faith is deepened.

I uplift and strengthen.

I support, not neglect.

I choose humility over pride and grace over knowledge.

I choose to be here, now while I wait for what is to come.

ABOUT ME RIGHT NOW

Currently...

Life is getting simpler.

My makeup routine consists of mascara, a quick brow touch-up, and some undereye concealer to brighten up the dark bags under my greens.

Priorities become fewer: my marriage, close friendships, then work.

I watch a sunset and sit on the floor with my husband laughing at our dogs—my current favorite recipe for contentment.

My work in following Jesus is less about the lines, rules, and proper scripture and more about loving God and others.

It's tempting to complexify really simple things.

Simple doesn't mean easy, and I think that gets confused.

"It's so simple!"

Simple is not quick and easy.

The Godly simple is really difficult.

It's so straightforward we have to place rules and religion around it because it cannot be that clear-cut and accessible.

But He's a God who died to make it clear cut. Again, not easy, but clear.

Here's the thing: He's already pleased with us.

From that pleasure, He invited us to partner with Him to first receive the love, then show it to others.

It doesn't make sense why He does it, or how.

We try our best to make sense of it, which is when we make it complex again.

There's no reason why I should get any kind of restart after the things I've done in my life.

No amount of logic could justify that.

Grace means the most when it doesn't make sense, and it's undeserved.

And that's our simple cue to know we're loving others; when it's not earned or given because we live a certain way or love a certain someone.

All that to say, I'm embracing a simpler life.

Oftentimes this brings pain, but it also brings an equal amount of joy and contentment.

Because the simple things are God's big things.

Like loving our neighbor and turning the other cheek. Like sunsets and the first sip of coffee.

The simple is the gift.

Hard to live out, but also glorious and gritty.

It's time to unlearn and relax into the love of God.

Let it envelop you as you surrender to the simple, still, small work of God.

UNPACKING

Take out. Unload. Empty. Uncrate.

BURNOUT MINISTRY

Ministry is a walking relationship with burnout.

It's not an "if" burnout will happen, it's a "when". And when it does, it often comes with fury. Passion is lost along with hope in God and mission.

I think this stems from the ludacris belief that ministry is to be 24/7, non-stop.

Ministry asks us to be ready at any time, any place, to help someone.

I don't have an issue with helping, but I do have an issue with this ministry model.

To me, it screams loud WE are the saviors.

ONLY we can take the phone calls at 3 am and respond to texts at home when we're with our families.
Whatever the need, it cannot wait! People's relationship with Jesus is on the line after all! When this is expected of you or your staff, you will experience burnout.

Perhaps this ministry model needs a new lens.

Since when did Jesus ask us to be the savior?

Was he on the cross, his chest heaving, saying, "Becki, only you can save these people"? No.

That's ridiculous.

And honestly, anti-Christ.

Those who are called to a full-time, vocational ministry need to take a step back and reevaluate.

Do we serve the need or God?

Do we serve the glory of ministry or being present with our kids and loving our partners? Do we serve the American-go-getter mission or one that requires a sabbath and rest?

I think you get that point.

Your first ministry will always be the one you put last on the list.

That's the way it works.

The stage is a dangerous lure.

The attention and lauding you're given for your work with kids, youth, young adults, leadership initiatives, arts, proposals, etc...
It makes you believe you hold high esteem and worth only in that space.

You make it a priority to fill your cup with the people in your work without even noticing it.

I am saying this because I struggle too.

Last time I checked, changing diapers doesn't make me feel high esteem and worth. It makes me tired.

Yet, home is the ministry.

It is the calling.

It is where our most important work happens.

Where we are transformed into the Christ-like through sacrifice, grace, and sleepless nights.

Jesus' upside-down kingdom isn't reserved only for parable examples.

Not only for the Samaritan women, the thief on the cross, or a lesson for Peter. It's for us. In church, at work, in our homes.

When we meet him face to face, will he say "Oh man, thanks for the long hours at the church" ? I'm not sure.

It may be along the lines of "I saw how you chose to love those I placed in your home and ordinary circumstances."

Let's get right, friends.

Home is the ministry.

BODY PARTS

I was challenged today by the reminder—the church is a body. Many parts, but one body.

Working in a church makes it easy to glaze over that certain passage of Scripture. It's easy to think one body part is more important than the other, maybe one has more leadership or direct purpose. Maybe one gets more attention or glory or money. Maybe one has a simple function.

Before I take this metaphor too far, I want to pause.

On my own body, I regularly focus on the parts I don't like over the ones that I do.

I focus on my stomach, hips, and thighs while forgetting my very mind is thinking these thoughts while pumping my heart's blood.

I forget, on the regular, how intricate and magical our bodies are.

My focus tends to be on what someone else has told me is unacceptable or undesiring, and ya know I do the same thing with my church body too.

At its best, it's a fantastic representation of God's love and power. At its worst, it's exclusive and political, and control-hungry.

And it is always at its worst and best in the same breath, just like us.

Our bodies are powerful because of the sum of their parts.

I think the point Jesus was trying to make in this analogy is that every part is so desperately needed to make the whole thing work.

Every belief, every race, every culture, and every tongue.

The flabby parts, the strong parts, and the ones we don't talk about.

Every single one of us is required to piece together this giant, radiant tapestry called the church—made up of stories and experiences. Hurt, triumph, and pain. True joy, deep calling, and purpose in our Monday-Friday.

My goodness, we lose so much of who we could be when we exclude.

When we draw lines and put up walls.

When we listen to the law over love.

One body, many parts.

The parts are gorgeously unique and diverse—to create the whole.

Let us not forget, though we have much to redeem and ask forgiveness for, the church is an intricate and magical specimen.

She's worth believing in.

IN LINE...WAITING

When the Israelites roamed in the wilderness for 40 years, they were supplied with manna from the sky. This manna would be enough to sustain them for only one day. If they tried to hoard it, as a means of security for the future, it would rot.

In my own wilderness, a few months into my 30s and conceiving journey, I find these verses stopping me in my tracks. Oh, how I love to plan for the future. I'm pretty great at telling God how I want to know exactly what and when in my timelines.

In my own way, I'm trying to gather manna for more than just today. Apps to track my cycles, Google to diagnose my symptoms, and overthinking every single wave of nausea or tiredness. I feel the push of not having enough time and the fear of being infertile just two months into this journey.

Yes, you read that right.

I expected to be pregnant the instant I got off birth control. After all, God willed it and promised it...right?

I also overlook the manna and choose something I can control, like fear and worry. I can just spin in anxious cycles instead of choosing to trust the manna will come. I should gather it, taste it and be grateful. Instead, I choose to worry whether manna will

The lesson in manna is provision for the present. God has given me all I need where I am, right now.

come tomorrow and ask God why the manna I have now isn't the kind I asked for. Or what I thought it would be.

The power of provision through manna cannot be seen unless I surrender my control. I also need to let the manna of today sustain me until tomorrow comes.

I can get grateful and focus on right now.

He will also give me what I need where I'll be when I hold my baby in my arms. When I get to see my husband as a dad and my dad as a grandpa.

When I cry with my crying baby out of sheer exhaustion and helplessness.

So, I thank you, God, for today's manna.

The sunshine and the beginning of fall.

The hope of your promise and the power of my present.

Thank you.

The lesson in manna is provision for the present. God has given me all I need where I am, right now.

GROCERY STORE GRIEF

Another encounter at the grocery store has left me feeling void of patience or compassion for those who approach me. I'm almost resentful toward them, interrupting my grocery mission with their hurt and pain regarding our pastor who is dying.

"You don't know me," I think.

"Just because I sing on a stage because I've been a face for 6 years —you don't know me."

Yesterday our lead pastor announced he was stepping down.

Though this is not a huge surprise, it still stings.

I wish I had more feelings about it, but I'm lost in my own.

Being so beyond done with ministry and this year...this news is just... another crisis to add to the last few working here.

However, I'm mourning a different idea.

Our pastor's mission is the one I signed up for. Every other leader set to help lead in the next season has a slight variation of it.

But one is too traditional, the other too high church.

I find myself, a believer, who fights for her relationship with God as an outsider.

I feel my guard being built, brick by brick—ones I've worked hard to tear down. But maybe it's my heart shutting to a place I know I can no longer stay.

I will be misunderstood.

My savior complex is begging me to stay.

Timing doesn't make sense, but it usually doesn't until much later. I'm needed and that is why I need to leave.

I scroll job pages numbly.

My feelings don't have names, but if I tried, I would say things like anger, bitterness, numbness, sadness, self-pity, anxiousness, and isolation.

Yet, hope. For what's next though it seems to be taking a while.

I'm sure and unsure with every second.

I'm tired.

Walter Brueggemann talks about transitions, surrender and endings by telling us our carefully crafted worlds can slowly be taken away.

Hard one to sit with.

Then he adds this is happening as a means of God's grace. God's goodness.

That is even harder to sit with.

And yet, in this moment I'm baking bread and listening to Ella Fitzgerald.

My house is clean while my dog's chest rises and falls. I begin to type slower soaking in presence.

Here's to transitions, slow and painful but quick and ruthless. God will guide me.

God holds me.

By the grace of God.

Right now, I just want to be a human.

Not a leader, or a church leader.

No boxes or behaviors—just me.

IDK, GOD

Listening to a podcast on a sabbath walk yesterday.

It hit me.

This right here is why Jesus tells us to love our neighbors, enemies, and everyone in between.

It's hard enough for them to accept love.

And usually our go-to is criticism, scripture references, and legality when ACTUALLY what is needed is empathy and human contact.

Those two traits will do more than referencing a verse in the Bible ever will.

They allow humanity.

They give permission and safety.

But why do we stop short of this love?

Could it be because we have not fully experienced or surrendered to the love of God? I haven't. I know it.

I'm still stuck in the cycle of earning love and favor.

Agreeing instead of standing up for what I believe in.

Choosing acceptance over the uncomfortable.

Thinking maybe my behavior and being "good" will land my spot in eternity. I'm missing the entire point.

I really believe we only know an ounce of the vast galaxy love of God.

And we like to think we have it figured out, don't we?

Who's in, who receives it, and who gets it only a little until they change their lifestyle or music taste.

God's love does not need to be "figured out".

It needs to be experienced by us to bring the changes all of us want to see.

Lately, I find myself just saying "I don't know" with God—about love, about following him and doing it "right."

God's love does not need to be "figured out". It needs to be experienced...

The gist is that an overwhelming majority people spend their whole lives struggling to believe God loves them...whether they are aware of it, or not.

We want a love that says I see you, instead of one that chastises our burdens.

We want a love that is actually unconditional, though it is uncomfortable to experience.

We want a love that sees past the guard we put up.

We want a love that hears our story first before giving advice or casting a judgment.

Ya know what? It's awkward, messy, and complex.

But it's also freeing.

It's forcing me to take a step back from certainty and see how much I bow down to it.

The only certainty I have is how much we don't know about God and his Love for this wild world.

And that is a good starting point for me.

'TIS THE SEASON

Another Sunday at home.

Slept in.

Yet I feel nagging guilt about not being in church.

Or even sitting down with my journal when I usually do.

My nagging dogma comes in and says "If you don't do this practice at this particular time, you're choosing sleep over God."

Why did I learn that? Why do we teach that?

Yes, following God requires sacrifice.

I'm writing about sacrifice from a place of ridiculous privilege.

However, somewhere along the way, I picked up that to be a Christian meant ONLY sacrifice and deed.

It meant early hours no matter the season.

It meant being away from your family more than being with them.

As I sit with this crusty theology on a Sunday in August, I get angry. So much to unlearn and relearn.

We really love to set up camp on the works side of things instead of sitting by the fire of faith. Yes, faith without works is dead. But works without faith...that may be worse.

It says "love your neighbor as yourself"--easy enough right? We all love ourselves so much....right?

I'm seeing how layered that passage really is.

The obvious point is preferring others as you prefer yourself.

Perhaps that is the foundation of knowing love, then being able to love others.

More so, being able to sleep in on a Sunday morning and trust God isn't disappointed with my choice, or that sleeping in means I'm not choosing him.

'Tis the season for unpacking bags, sorting through the mounds of feelings, and finding God in the process.

Does God not desire rest for us?

Does he not do his best and most sharpening work in our very homes?

But the deeper layer begins with receiving the love of God as you are.

Full of sin, full of brilliance. We are loved in this place, as we are.

ABOUT ME RIGHT NOW

I find myself in the final week of the year, the endless black hole of holiday cookies, late bedtimes, and a house that has thrown up toys. My anxiety is at its peak, being out of routine and having a go-go-go schedule.

I have a one-year-old.

I have been a parent for over a year.

I struggle between loving her so fiercely and being afraid of what I'll do to her as her mom. I don't like not knowing things and parenthood is one giant lesson in it.

My marriage is different and I struggle to let seasons come and go.

The fresh-parent stage is new to us.

It's a stark reminder of how much freedom we actually had before having our daughter. I don't have much to complain about, I just miss the ease of us and the freedom.

It's about intention right now.

Sometimes we get it right, other times we don't.

I spent years wanting someone to see me and let me lead and champion something. Now the opportunity is in my lap and I resist it.

My obsession with independence and only helping others is sky-high right now. I don't know how to tell my friends or husband I need help.

I don't even know how to figure that out myself.
Just because I can do it all, doesn't mean I have to.

I don't know if I'll ever get that one right.

I wonder if I'm truly loved, all of me. It's a struggle to receive it.

I come alive teaching in the classroom.

I'm ready to learn and grow as a teacher...in the classroom, on stage, on social, and in my life. The thing is, I struggle with being placed in seasons of learning...ones that make me better.

Church is still weird for me.

I'm guarded yet cautiously open.

I receive worship and cry through it.

There's something so safe about it, every time.

God is simply love and comfort and peace.

I'm being reminded of how powerful the expression of worship is.

It's wildly critiqued, complex, and made more complicated than it needs to be because of that power.

I'm coming off of a WILD year, one I never saw coming in every way.

I wonder what this year will bring.

It's changed me.

Parts of me have been severed.

There's new budding growth.

There's still chaff to burn away.

Yet the foundation remains.

I'M TIRED OF MY LIFE RIGHT NOW

I have these weeks where I just get tired of my life.

I'm sick of rushing around.

I feel guilt and shame for being away from my kid so much.

The days when I come home and the countertops are cluttered with dishes in the sink, and the dog whining–it's a lot right now.

Sprinkle in doing work that feels lifeless–I'm frustrated, tired, and anxious.

It's okay if life feels heavy. Even plates full of God's gifts can be heavy...but it says his yoke is easy and his burden is light.

When I'm away from my kid, she's bonding and blessing my husband and my parents. When I come home to chaos, it's a home that is lived in and well-loved.

When I feel overextended and tired, stop and cancel.

Be unapologetic.

The work I'm doing isn't my identity or what makes life worth anything.

It's okay to be overwhelmed and not love the work.

It's right to feel the sparkle of knowing it's not what you're set on earth to do.

I can hold it all because God can.

Trust.

There are good things to learn here, too–in the tired weeks. God is with us.

Be at peace.

A FEW THOUGHTS ON CALLING

My understanding of calling always came with flashing lights, loud booms, and clear concise instructions from God.

I expected to know I was in this calling while also doing it.

I thought I knew all the ways calling worked, the seasons and locations, and the people that embodied said calling.

All of that can be true.

But here's my experience with it...

My "calling" involved me stumbling into ministry. Discovering I liked it.

Understanding it made something come alive within me.

I'm learning my calling is multi-faceted, not just one clear-cut path.

It is equally filled with proposals, teaching, dirty diapers, and breakdowns.

The work you do that lasts and matters usually ends up being the least sexy.

I have callings I still run from, and callings that were never mine to pursue. It's complex.

And I wonder if we're supposed to "know".
I wonder if a life surrendered to Jesus does not contain just one call.

The job that pays you may very well not be your calling.

The work you do that lasts and matters usually ends up being the least sexy.

It lies in the rigid ordinary.

Who you spend time with, who you have relationships with, serving people, and making a living.

There are callings I sign up for with my faith and ones that are within and flow out of me with ease.

There are callings other people place on me.

There are callings I place on myself.

So which one wins? Which one honors God?

They all do.

If your life is like mine, sometimes every hour brings different work.

So, I kind of think it's silly to search for a calling when it lies in and all around us.

God isn't someone who hides when we call out to him... He's not a jerk.

If your theology involves God being a jerk, it's time to move towards some better theology.

"The earth is filled with his glory"...classic 2000's worship. But also, that's some hopeful theology.

For me, that means literally everything points back to God and draws us back to him. Isn't that what calling is?

Isn't that the point?

Maybe it doesn't have to be a big ole event with high attendance and followers. Maybe it can be your ordinary day, being aware and surrendered to God's call.

Maybe we can just be responsive...

What if that's all it took?

THE COOL KIDS...AND ME.

There's been a space I've been in for over a year.

It's snuck into my thoughts and worth, leaving me questioning my identity. Asking if who I am/what I am/what I value is enough.

I was invited into this circle.

I've never felt like I could fully be a part.

Here, my body feels too mushy and curvy.

The food I brought was not perfectly staged. The wine, not top shelf. My heart wasn't enough.

My house wasn't enough.

My life felt too messy.

My heart felt too open.

As I slowly release my grip, take a step back, and trust my knowing (that has been there for a year, plus my husband's as well)...I've decided I'm proud of who I am. ESPECIALLY in spaces I don't feel I belong.

I am a boxed-wine-loving, mushy-body-wearing, wrinkle-age-embracing human. The food I bring to parties is from the store or Pinterest OR I get extravagant with it.

I value presence over boasting life over social feeds AND I celebrate my life over those social feeds. I'm about the hard stuff and deeper meaning.
I love to laugh and feel comfortable and free in my friend's presence.

I love spaces where I'm free...and I haven't been letting myself be.

So, I take some time away.

People cannot hold all of me like I want them to.

So, I say goodbye and hello to more life. To remembering me.

Sincerity.

Tired eyes.

Lowering facade

Embracing chaos.

Holding boundaries for my Knowing.

It's not forever.

I'll return.

But let's normalize taking time to remember who we are.

We don't need to mold and bend to other people's preferences. In fact, it's a tragedy when we succumb to that.

Remember your people.

Remember who you are.

Remember, you are not supposed to fit into those boxes with empty promises of belonging.

I THOUGHT OBEDIENCE WOULD BE SEXIER...

Obedience has held the same stance in my mind as submission.

My response has always been, "Don't tell me what to do".

I've heard this word paired with submission as a power tactic for a lot of my life, especially in Christian culture, so I've considered myself above it.

Well, when I met my husband, that changed.

See, true and good obedience's fruit is submission.

And submission is not weakness; it is serving one another.

I submit to whatever my husband wants because he controls the house. Just kidding, not even close.

But I do submit to Joel—I know, every feminist just died. The cool thing?

Joel also submits to me.

Who knew?! It's about loving and serving each other in obedience. Ebb and flow, man.

Sure, there are power struggles, because everyone thinks they're right.

Everyone's obedience and submission look different.

Right now, I seem to be in a season of waiting and obedience.

But it's not cool obedience, like leaving your good-paying job to pursue your new start-up. Nor is it getting pregnant.

Nor is it moving across the country to start new or experience a new city and its inhabitants.

No, my obedience looks like going to work every day.

It looks like a partnership with my husband and constantly examining my motives. It looks like trusting God has plans.

It looks like trusting God's timing over mine, which is so hard.

I find myself being surrounded by people who get "sexy obedience".

The big, life-altering change instead of waking up every day and doing the same thing.

Here's the thing though: there are seasons of both. Obedience is never sexy, but it is a partnership.

I guess a good way to look at it is when you're dating/engaged.

Everything is so new and exciting, and it's sexy because you are so passionately in love with the other person.

Then marriage comes, and in my experience, you slowly evolve into being roommates with benefits.

And I'm here to say, that's not a bad thing—in fact, it's gorgeous.

I've become good friends with my husband, I like him, and I love him—even though he could pick up after himself a bit more.

Here's the quote that's rocking my world lately:

"Life gets very quiet before all the doors open. I'm learning that what can feel like loneliness is actually grace. REST. Find your strength, it will all change soon" -J. Lynn

Obedience applies here, too.

Grace and rest are possible in obedience. In fact, they are necessary.

So, whether your obedience is sexy or ordinary, keep showing up to it.

God has good things ahead.

He has not left you in this place, nor will he change his mind about you.

You are exactly where you need to be.

Obedience is the same.

Passionate when it's new, but takes more intentionality when you settle into it.

It requires some grit, and as a highly emotional person—letting some logic and sense in.

LOVE YOUR ENEMIES & OTHER HARD THINGS

"You're familiar with the old written law, 'Love your friend,' and its unwritten companion, 'Hate your enemy.' I'm challenging that. I'm telling you to love your enemies. Let them bring out the best in you, not the worst."
Matthew 5:44 MSG

I've never considered myself one to have enemies.

My former description of an enemy was anyone I wanted to kill, or worse, anyone who wanted to kill or hurt me.

When scripture would describe enemies, I would immediately go literal.

The bad guys and bad people—love them.

Yes, true dat.

However, I'm learning your enemy is actually someone who you feel attacked by. Sure, physically, but for now I'm talking mentally and spiritually.

Someone who takes cheap shots at you.

Someone who thinks they are above you and others.

The dang Democrat who keeps pushing his agenda on you. The pro-lifer thinks the pro-choicer is wrong and visa versa.

Your enemy can be anyone.

Especially the person you hope you never become.

We all have examples in our life of people who we learned what NOT to do from. Toxic people focused on self and self only.

Recently I've been learning another layer of what "love your enemies" means.

See, I have someone who I consider now to be my enemy.

And I've done work with Jesus on it, but the name alone brings back lots of memories of being put down on the regular.

Nothing I could do was right or good and they made sure I knew that. So, of course, I make the vow to never be like that ever.

My pride says, "I would NEVER do that".

Yeah well, I did.

I will again. And so will you.

See, the "love" mentioned is rooted in humility.

Humility is understanding you are not better than anyone.

Humility here is understanding you have the same capacity to hurt someone, just like your enemy.

Humility understands that I'm only one situation or circumstance away from being in the same place my enemy is in, one which shaped them and maybe their reactions to me.

In understanding I had the same gross traits as my enemy, I gained empathy and grace. It's easier to get to a negative place than we think it is.

It's harder to fight against it and coexist with empathy for each other.

> *Humility understands that I'm only one situation or circumstance away from being in the same place my enemy is in...*

I have made a lot of points, but I wanted to point out a time I thought I "knew" what this passage and mantra meant. And sure, I can know in my head what it means.
It's another thing totally to get to a place of seeing how enemy-like you've become and how capable you are of getting to that place.

The end of the verse says, "Let them bring out the best in you".

Your best isn't necessarily resurrection or a conflict-free relationship. It could be choosing to extend grace.

It could be stooping low and asking for forgiveness.

It could be empathy for your enemy's story.

Love your enemies, in doing so, you bring out the best in yourself.

TRANSITIONS

Transition is separation.

I don't like when people glaze over how difficult it is.

The transition from one season, relationship, or career to the next.

Turning the page in a sense.

Trying hard to be grateful for the chapter written, but clinging onto it with white knuckles. Even the hard can be comfortable if it's all we've known.

I've had some hard years in my work life.

Ripping apart some dreams.

Saying goodbye, very slowly, to a place I thought I belonged. Where I wanted to be.

The transition isn't instant.

It's slow and steady.

With every rejection comes understanding and grieving...that (dreams, hopes, community, etc) won't happen here.

When the transition isn't instant, I try to rewrite the story.

I keep my grip, grab a chisel and build something new—clinging onto what I wanted.

So, every day is a slow death to what is known and waking up to what's unknown.

I think this is how we're supposed to live our life, but it's hard.

I'm not good at the tension of both, I like to live fully on one side or the other. We are complex enough to navigate the tension with God.

He stills my emotions and fears—never making me feel irrational or dumb. He gets me.

So, on another day of transition, I do the same. This is not all I am, here, now.

I'm becoming who I am here, now.

But it is not the end.

So, I write the final words of this chapter, eagerly waiting for the next.

Trusting. Having faith. Letting go.

Transition is surrender, in God's eyes.

Letting go. Embracing. Being complicated, not knowing the ending but saying yes anyway.

OBSESSIVE-OVERCOMER

What is it in the Christian faith, or even Christian culture that is obsessed with being the overcomer?

I'm not so sure struggles are supposed to be met with the overcoming- I'll-beast-this-trial, posture.

If we look at the stories of scripture, we often see our characters running from their issues or sitting down with God, questioning how to proceed. I relate to that a lot more than sweeping statements about God being bigger than the struggle and lyrical battle cries of declaration...quickly declaring God's goodness instead of sitting with the pain created to be our teacher and guide.

Maybe I have more of an issue with confronting every issue with a need to OVERCOME it. That sounds exhausting from the start.

It doesn't feel like there is room for fear or feeling insecure or worthless...when those feelings have A LOT to teach us about what we believe. About ourselves. Our faith. Our God...

He cried out to God in his anguish while also trusting the cup given to him.

So when we encounter these bumps or total train wrecks in our lives, it cannot just be something to "overcome."

It must be something to walk through, letting the pain and complexity of it all have its way with us. It is not until this path is forged we can truly see the fruit and design of overcoming.

And can I be honest?

I think the world is tired of abrasive Christians who declare more than they care.

> ## I've seen the devastation that moving too quickly and triumphantly through hard seasons can bring.

It's easy to sit on a throne of our own translations and denominational bylaws, all wrapped in a box built from control, shouting about who God is. But don't you see how the world reels back from this uppercut type of communication from Christians?

I've seen the devastation that moving too quickly and triumphantly through hard seasons can bring. We need to remember that our own Christ grieved and wept in his journey to be our overcomer.

I truly think and believe (head and heart, y'all) that the way forward requires us to hold more openness to pain and hardship. To the cries of people experiencing it. It's going to require us to step out of our perfectly curated answers to the "ways of the world" and into our actual pain.

The good news is Jesus is already there, waiting to meet us.

And he will help us overcome...but it won't be in the way we think.

This overcoming feels like a prodigal coming home.

Like being held when you feel small.

This overcoming won't always be big and bright, it will require little steps and childlike faith.

It will feel like a return to yourself, in turn, a return to Love and light.

This is what it is to overcome.

To overcome is not a battle cry.

It's a birthing cry.

Resilient.

Trusting.

Birthing new life from pain.

87

UNFOLDING

The "ability to develop oneself in any way one desires".

ONCE-A-MONTH-FRIENDS

I went on a walk with my closest friend this morning.

She arrived, I made coffee, and our sleepy eyes went on a walk together.

We've both lived a lot of life and hurt over the past four years of our friendship. Single life, quitting jobs, getting married, and being in relationships.

I think it's a beautiful thing to be in this kind of friendship.

I used to think people who held tight to their friend groups were rude and uninviting. Now, we both get it.

The time and energy you put into your closest friends is good and holy.

The space you give to your acquaintances and once-a-month coffee friends is also holy.

I believe Jesus had both.

I think there's a flaw in Christians thinking you cannot cut people out because it's not Christlike.

I learned the hard way, a couple of different times: people are not usually in our lives forever. They are often used in seasons, to prepare us or to show up some truth.

I had two close friendships dissolve when I got married, and ya know what? It was devastating. I'd never had a loss in my life like that. It was public, it was 100% a friend breakup.

But, their exit made room for others to step into my life, ones that I NEEDED in this season of marriage. And I fully believe my exit made room for more beauty in theirs too.

Being a people pleaser and "IS EVERYONE HAPPY OK GOOD THEN I'M HAPPY" type, I've been learning this the hard way.

To help, I sat down with the Voice that matters and asked who was supposed to get the most out of my time and energy now that I had become a wife and relationships looked different. He gave me the name of people in my life, and those have taken priority.

YES, I still get coffee with the every-once-in-awhile people.

So, clinging to relationships or saying yes to everyone who needs you isn't Christlike, unless you feel strongly it's within your lane to be close to them. If you cannot give a person a good dose of your energy and time, I'd think twice about answering their text to grab a coffee.

You do not have to do it all, friend.

You are not in control of how and if people meet Jesus.

Jesus mentioned 12 followers, though he had many.

Within his followers, he had mentions of only a few.

When he healed someone, he left them—trusting them to God.

He didn't try to pursue a relationship, even when they asked him for more.

May we trust him enough to do the same.

AN ODE TO MY TWENTIES

As I get ready to cap off the pervious ten years of my life, I'm grateful to say I can leave them with mixed emotions.

I made so many mistakes and hurt so many people.

I had to unlearn priorities to learn healthy ones.

I healed. I grew and grew up.

I lived in my apartment alone, filled with eclectic décor from goodwill and kind friends.

I gained a pup and learned that all dogs are not golden retrievers... especially German short-haired pointers.

I learned where my voice is needed, and equally so, how powerful it can be.

I sing for a living—how wild is that?

I began the journey of marriage on a cold, dreamy beach— exchanging vows we knew would be hard to live out each day— but knowing it was worth trying.

My faith got simpler and God got bigger.

I lost friends and gained ones needed for each season I walked through.

I began walking with anxiety and am learning every day to sit and listen to what it's telling me instead of letting it drag me around

I lived in tents, single-bedroom apartments, houses with roommates, and a home in the suburbs.

I've had every hairstyle in the book and struggled with body image.

Also, that never goes away—but I have landed on the desire to be healthy and to look and feel like me.

Simpler the better—in all areas of life.

31 THINGS I LEARNED IN MY TWENTIES

- Presence is power. Do not spend all your time worrying about the future because everything can change in 4 months or 4 years.

- While single, I learned how to listen to my heart and mind. I learned WHO I WAS and what I stood for. I learned how to love others and also myself. I learned I wasn't put on this earth to wish for others to love me, but rather to go love others. And myself, too.

- My faith was untamed, finding its grounding in simple truths without all the rules. In doing so, God got a whole lot bigger.

- I'm created to be a bridge builder.

- Relationships are seasonal. And just because they end, it doesn't mean you've failed.

- Sometimes, people are in your life for the seasons you need them. Always learning this one.

- Be weird.

- Anxiety is always telling me something I'm afraid of or a lie I'm believing, but it is not of God. I'm trying to sit with it and listen instead of running away or wasting time believing its lies. Ways I fight: practice presence, say a prayer, share how you're feeling with someone you trust, and get active.

- Surround yourselves with people that think and believe differently than you. This makes your faith personal because you have a face to a stereotype. A name for the "lost soul". You find quickly, God loves them just as much as He loves you.

- Buy yourself fresh flowers.

- Saying no is holy and good.

- Surround yourself with people who are better than you at your craft/profession. Learn and grow in humility—lifting others while not questioning your worth.

- Be hopeful and joyful, even if you're conceived as immature and naive.

- Every human being just wants to be told they're loved and accepted for who they are.

- Talk to God every day.

- Everything is sacred—people, coffee, sunshine, and work meetings.

- My body is a temple—healthy and strong. Turn the page on body insecurity and what society tells you to look like--move towards body appreciation and health.

- Submission and obedience are beautiful in a healthy context.

- Anything you experience that feels like the end of the world, remember it is not. You will make it through, and you will grow from it.

- NOTHING is wasted. No ordinary day, hard season, thriving season—all is redeemed in its time.

- Speak your truth, but remember your speaking to another human who cares about their own truth too.

- Feelings are valid. Emotions are not a burden or something that makes you "too much". It is good and holy to be sensitive.

- Your relationship with God is unique, just like you. Therefore, how it plays out will be unique too. That's what makes it beautiful.

- Say yes to a big, scary adventure. Mine? Moving to a different state, getting married, working in ministry, choosing to believe in God outside of my upbringing, etc...

- God wants good for you.

- Cultivate fierce hope. For yourself. Others. The world around you.

- I'm living my best life when I eat chips in my bed.

- Find ways to belly laugh.

- I don't like to be told what to do, but sometimes I need it from those I trust.

- Everyone and everything has something to teach you if you'll allow it.

- Finding people that speak what your heart is feeling is one of the holiest things on this earth.

PRODIGAL

As I reflect on this story, I picture myself leaving home.

I'm not running away, pockets full of money, ready to raise hell.

No, I'm walking. A light is on in the house, as it always is.

Day and night, the light streams through the window.

I make camp in the hills, under the stars.

I go into towns, befriending people that make me feel less alone. People I eat meals with and talk through life's greatest mysteries.

I work in the fields; sowing and harvesting what has been planted.

I'm gone for a while.

Inside my heart feels a tug towards that light in the window. I simply tell it to think about the tasks of the next day.

My mind wanders towards home daily, yet I do not return.

I find purpose in the work I'm doing and the people that surround me.

It's not that I don't believe in Home, no not at all.

It's because I believe in Home that I've left.

But the light in the window—it's hard for me to understand why it is always on. Why doesn't He turn it off?

Being away begins to feel too heavy, and I make the journey to return.

The memories of Home make me feel warm, and I'd like to feel warm again.

It feels like the wandering I had done mattered.

As I approach my home, I see a warm glow in the distance. It's the light left on—in the day and night.

My tired eyes and body remember with every step what Home feels like. It feels like a warm embrace.

It feels like the wandering I had done mattered.

It felt familiar and also too good to be true.

As I reached the doorway, a quiet voice inside whispered,

"The light is always on so you can always find your way back home.

It glows to remind you that love lives here and within, even though you may leave.

Day or night, it stays—my message to you is that I stay. "

It's not that I don't believe in Home, no not at all. It's because I believe in Home that I've left.

"I know you need to leave sometimes to make sense of Home, so I leave the light on."

I walk into the house.

We sit down at the table and talk about my journey.

The light in the window glows as the sun paints the sky, settling in for the night.

For this moment, I am Home.

THANK GOD FOR THIS

I'm in month 6 of my pregnancy.

I now feel baby kicks, growing more intense every day as she grows. I sang to her for the first time this week.

Prayed out loud, and talked to her.

If I'm honest, my mind is making this pregnancy hard. Everything else—it's beautiful.

But I worry.

Will I love her enough?

Will the connection be there?

Will Joel connect with her?

What if I love her more than him?

I don't know if I'm ready to give up my marriage dynamic right now. All I see and hear around me is how kids make everything harder.

Yet no one remembers what it was like to be preparing for this reality.

More so, I've never prepared for this reality.

I wish I felt more faith than fear. But I'm working on that.

Once again, God asks me to trust.

He asks me to remember He doesn't call without promise. He will never leave.

This is His gift, so why would it bring destruction?

It will certainly bring refining.

But yet, we're called to the present as we prepare for the future. So today...

I heard baby girl's heart.

135 beats per minute, in perfect rhythm.

It's the tempo for her kicks, growing stronger by the day.

She loves dancing after food, just like me.

She likes to hide from Dad but gives him a kick every once in a while.

Little love, you're already changing me.

Your dad and I love you.

It's an odd thing to prepare for your world to be turned upside down.

It's difficult to swallow. You will be different. I will be different. WE will be different.

We're in awe that we get to add you to our little family. You'll love your fur sisters.

Thank you, God, for this.

I do not know to what extent I can be thankful yet, but I am. And I can be thankful and anxious at the same time.

God of the *and.*

LET'S GO OUTSIDE

I find myself sad with Christianity, a lot.

I push against the church.

I feel on the outside of it all, and honestly? I like it here.

I've been in the inner workings. I've been praised and elevated on the inside. Out here though, it's quieter; but more clear than ever.

In yet another wandering season, God is my Home, not the church.

Maybe it's not forever, but I'll trust God will move me when it's needed.

Sometimes you have had to fight and strive for what God intends. I think you do need to surrender to a timeline other than your own so dreams find their place eventually.

I'm trying to be less of a savior.

To get okay with letting people down.

To say no to good things, too.

I'm trying to be wholehearted, unboxing parts and beliefs I've hidden.

I'm learning to receive the good and the bad and the unthinkable, too.

Learning boundaries is like grace and forgiveness–freeing but requires sacrifice.

On this Sunday in June, I'm held as I learn and grow.

You are, too.

DO YOU WANT TO BE WELL?

This story from the Bible hits differently in this season of life and in this world we live in. Jesus is asking this man who has been in this spot for years, "Do you want to be well?"

Usually, it is the ones begging for healing we find ourselves identifying with. But I identify with this guy.

In my experience, when Jesus asks if I want to be well, he's offering another way.

I tend to pack my bag of self-righteousness pretty full. Some of it is righteous anger, and some of it is me elevating myself, pretending I don't have the characteristics I loathe in others.

Spoiler, I do.

I often take the path of bitterness and criticism. I often fail to give those who have hurt me any sort of second chance or forgiveness.

I cling tight to my hurt and make it a part of my identity, thinking it makes me unique and different.

I chose to put my head down and count every step instead of lifting my face to feel the sunshine.

Jesus asks, "Do you want to be well?"

I'm not sure.

What is stripped away by being "well" leaves me feeling naked and soft. It feels like they (whoever they are) have won.

Do you want to be well?

I exhale.

I do.

I do want to be well.

See, when Jesus asks this question, I think he's asking us what our source is. Is our source our hurt, anger, and past?

No matter how valid the pain is I think he's asking us to surrender it. He's asking us to give him a chance at making us well.

And maybe when we say yes, a load feels like it's lifted off, though nothing is different. The person still rejected you.

The job still fired you.

The pain you feel still lives in you.

Your thoughts are still dark.

But....

That person who rejected you doesn't get the final say.

The job that fired you opened doors for a better one.

The pain you feel still lives in you, but it's held by grace and understanding.

Your thoughts are still dark but something is also there, helping you remember you're not alone.

Do you want to be well?

Do *you* want to be well?

Yes, at the end of the day, I do. Even though it makes me feel naked and soft. Perhaps that's the way it's supposed to be.

I don't think it's a 180 turnaround, black-and-white thing.

I think it's moving our eyes from the ground to the sky.

I think it's giving other people a chance again.

I think it's telling God about our weariness and letting him hold us.

I'M OVER IT

Can I be honest? Sometimes healing sucks.

I make choices every day to uplift an organization full of people who gave up on me. It's weird because some days it's easy.

Other days, it makes me want to rip my hair out and burn everything down.

A dear friend got to find a resolution with leadership. She was heard and seen.

I loved that for her.

I'm sad for me.

One of the hardest parts of healing for me is letting myself be mad and frustrated and acknowledging I was hurt.

Because I'm not innocent, I know I'm not.

I think if I let myself feel the brevity of it all again, I would go into a hole it would take me a while to get out of.

In my current work, I cannot exist in a bitter place.

So, I focus on rebuilding instead of the lingering feelings and baggage.

Most days, it's helpful. On other days, it feels like I'm lying.

> ## Healing forces us to put down the facade and projections we strut around with and show up to our days as ourselves.

If you are feeling sad, sit with it.

If you're angry, vent to someone you love.

If you're at peace, stop questioning and just let yourself rest.

It's endlessly complex and layered...yet healing encompasses what it means to be fully human. Healing is us at our best, the most honest version of ourselves.

Healing forces us to put down the facade and projections we strut around with and show up to our days as ourselves.

Healing is humbling, knocking us off our soapboxes.

What is it to truly move on?

I think it's allowing yourself to be where you're at every day.

I'm not sure we ever move on, fully.

Maybe that hurt or death or interaction is just another patch on our cub scout vest for being human and whole.

It isn't our identity.

Rather, it has made us softer...more fully alive.

Maybe that's the point.

THURSDAY NIGHTS

And sometimes, Thursday nights are the most beautiful thing you could have imagined.

One where cameras can't quite capture the sky or the presence I feel as I walk my daughter around our neighborhood.

The perfection of Ari's voice saying, "More nuggies mommy" while she focuses on drawing and creating in her own little world and stuffing her face.

The peace that comes after realizing you actually don't need to do it all.

Watching fall turn and show off in our new neighborhood, remembering the moments I wished for this.

Soaking up the last bit of daylight with a stroller ride, basking in a perfect milky sky, accentuating the brilliant colors of fall.

Life is chaos. Man, is it wild. And maybe that's the point.

I don't think we'll ever "arrive" or "know"...

We won't reach a spot where we have it all together.

And maybe that is the point.

GLORY

How many times do we participate, unknowingly, in the glory of God?

An unexpected sick day at home with your kid.

Accepting that phone call.

Letting someone merge in traffic.

Sending a text telling someone you're thinking of them.

Engaging in a work meeting.

Holding your kid's hand during breakfast.

Saying hello in the parking lot.

I think I believe, still, God's will is big and booming.

From a call, to a word, to the Gospel message we are a part of.

It's big and grand and gorgeous.

It's contained in small moments and quiet yeses.

God doesn't belong to only the grand.

He belongs also to the ant and bird.

To the whale and cliffs.

To the mountains and that feeling we have when we take them in.

This week, we participate in God's glory. In every little action.

Whatever it is, he's in it all.

A NOTE ON MY THERAPY JOURNEY

We love the metamorphosis metaphor.

Staying neatly tucked away in a cocoon until we reemerge as a perfect butterfly, flying away.

But in the cocoon, there is death, rebirth, and new life. It's gooey, suffocating, and vulnerable.

But perhaps that is the strength that causes this butterfly to be able to dance in the wind.

I feel like I'm reintroducing myself.

After years of wriggling around in my cocoon, whether it was forced or impending, despite all attempts to get out early...here I am, peeking through with newly formed wings.

Unused.

But I'm ready.

I'm not sure it's time for flight, yet.

But I'm committed to the transformation and the time it must take.

The flight will be free because of the dedication to my present.

Today I embrace the "not yet".

Being more gentle with past-me.

Believing in future me.

ORDINARY BRAVERY

I'm taking back the word brave.

It's paired with grandiose events and intellectual people.

But I believe it takes bravery to live in the ordinary.

The mundane, day-to-day.

I've assembled the following examples of bravery based on the people I live next to:

Sometimes bravery looks like getting out of bed in the morning.

Choosing to put one foot in front of the other when your world is crumbling around you. The world keeps spinning and your heart is tired and it's hard to muster up the strength to just be.

Sometimes bravery looks like raising a family.

Being asked/forced to constantly put your own needs on the back burner.

Smiling through tired eyes at your kiddos despite only sleeping 1-3 hours a night. Teaching these little people how to be decent human beings through discipline, learning, and love. Not only that but finding joy in them.

Sometimes bravery looks like being in love with your spouse.

Choosing to love one another deeply. To be a constant companion, someone to walk through ups and downs with. Continually choosing them, even though it can be difficult.

Sometimes bravery looks like asking the one person that everyone thinks you should be friends with to coffee.

You know, the one you think is too cool to be friends with you? Not only going to coffee but talking about things that matter.

Sometimes bravery looks like letting go of _____.

You name it. Relationships, your favorite unhealthy food, ego, shortcomings.

Sometimes bravery looks like searching.

Continuing to walk into the unclear and gray areas. When everyone else sees in black and white, having the courage to ask questions that make people uncomfortable. That make you uncomfortable.

Sometimes bravery looks like admitting you're wrong.

Choosing a relationship over the need to be right. Over pride of looking foolish.

Sometimes bravery looks like waiting.

Choosing to be fully present while you're waiting for something. A promise to be fulfilled. Choosing to worship and stay engaged.

Sometimes bravery looks like being present.

Choosing to stay and experience the now, instead of rushing to the next event, meeting, or cup of coffee.

Sometimes bravery is loving people even though they let you down.

To be hurt means that you have love in your heart. For my friends that love Jesus, it means He exists there.

Sometimes bravery means being the bigger person.

Even though you've been wronged, hurt, or maybe even taken advantage of. Everything in you wants to retaliate and make the other suffer. But you don't. You lean towards humanity. You lean toward grace.

Sometimes bravery means being fully yourself.

No matter what anyone else tells you or makes you feel or think; the gift to this world is who you are. Your likes, dislikes, passions, humor, laughs, and frown lines.

Sometimes bravery means redeeming baggage.

Experiences stay with us. Use it. Learn from it.

Sometimes bravery means letting people love you.

Not just brushing off a kind word. Daring to believe that it just may be true and that maybe...just maybe that's how people view you. Not with the distorted lenses you view yourself with.

Sometimes bravery looks like choosing forgiveness.

I don't believe forgiveness truly begins until you walk in it every day and pray for the person that hurt you.

Sometimes bravery is simply admitting you're brave in the ordinary.

Choose to dig your feet in, and love the people around you that drive you nuts.

To embrace whatever season you're in and learn from it.

To be fully human, taking the good days with the bad.

Learning to love yourself and embrace your character.

To feed your soul with good books, and green pastures.

To let your heart break, feel brokenness deeply, and be moved to action.

To celebrate that problem area on your body that really is your best feature.

To live in the present and experience the richness of life in the ordinary.

Oh friends, let's be brave.

FRIENDSHIPS AND ENDSHIPS

I've been lucky.

I count myself #blessed when it comes to deep and meaningful friendships.

Something that I could have never seen though? Not staying BFF's for life with those I was BFF's with.

I've got baggage with the phrase "best friend".

Maybe it's because I feel it excludes other friends, telling them they are good but not the *best*. Maybe it's because some of the people who held that title in my life do not carry it anymore. Maybe it's because I always want to be everyone's best friend but get sad when I'm not theirs. As you can see, it's complicated.

I'm here to talk to you about seasons and the ebb and flow of friendship relationships in our lives.

To help us all hold our friendships open-handed.

Maybe it'll help us know a relationship is always two parts; double the help and double the hurt.

I met one of my best friends in college. We were distant at first, then realized we are both hilarious and theatre junkies.

The rest was history.

Choir tours and trips to her hometown.

When her family moved to Florida, we went down for spring break. We graduated college and lived together as roommates.

We went to church together and served on the vocal team.

We were thick as thieves until we weren't.

A boy came into the picture, she chose him.

I was devastated. And of course I was adamant it was all her fault and not mine.

Later on, a boy came into my life and I understood what happened.

I lost another close friend as I chose my own boy.

It's funny when grace happens. When life twists you around a bit and literally puts you in the shoes of the person who has hurt you.

Fast forward a few painful years filled with awkward encounters, game night attempts, and text apologies later...we find ourselves here.

Separate lives, wishing nothing but deep happiness for each other.

When we fell out, it was devastating. The earth shook and everyone thought Jesus was returning. Nope. Just a couple of girls in their early twenties ending a friendship.

The pain of a lost friendship is also a teacher.

I see now with clarity how much I needed her.

She prepared me for marriage and taught me how to see and love people who would rather stay in on a Friday night and do a puzzle.

I learned the value of listening.

I learned how to be in the same lane, talent-wise, with a close friend.

I learned how difficult it is to lead close friends who happen to be on your volunteer teams.

I'm sure she learned things from me too, but I'm not sure I'll ever know them.

My point? Seasons, y'all.

My life could not be the way it is right now if she still was in it.

There would be no room for my sister-in-law who happens to be one of my closest friends. No room for new couple friends.

No room for another friendship that blossomed out of the hurt both of us shared.

I count myself lucky to have experienced the full circle of redemption.

I know that's not always the case.

And I know people say and do unspeakably terrible things to each other.

But pain's invitation still stands.

If you're in the middle of a friendship on the rocks, I empathize.

It was one of the hardest things I've ever gone through in my 30 years. It was almost like a divorce—for her and I. For the people around us.

This is the phrase I clung to:
"God's heart is always redemption".

Redemption can look different and unique to each person and situation.

For us, it's genuine love and gratitude for what we learned from each other—the bad and good. For others, it may look like deleting their phone number.

It may be choosing forgiveness 100x times a day, especially when the other party shows no interest in admitting they have failed you.

It may look like examining your own heart, admitting where some of the ugly parts of you showed.

No matter what form it takes, it's necessary.

To be able to move on, you must do the hard work of healing. The weight is yours to hold and who you give it to matters.

The pain of a lost friendship is also a teacher.

It's an invitation to so many inward lessons waiting to be learned.

It's practice for saying goodbye to loved ones.

It's humility and grace lessons.

It's a school of what true forgiveness looks like.

Though you hold it, you do not need to carry it.

The Arms of Grace bring the strength to find redemption in the mess.

So, cheers to friendships and endships and finding what redemption means in every single facet.

SHIFTING

I remember a day when I used to be more excited to come to work than be home.

Leaving here was almost impossible.

I wanted to be at every rehearsal, every meeting.

I felt valued and also like I couldn't miss anything.
It was a beautiful, busy season.

It's a big reason why I am on staff now. Why I'm trusted and proven loyal.

However, today I can't wait to get home. I'm not sure that's a bad thing.

It feels a bit full circle-like.

Maybe even healthy.

I love this work, but it is not who I am, nor what gets everything.

It is a part of my life, but not my whole life as it was before.

Sure, there are harder reasons why.

But I'm also choosing to get content with better reasons.

My friendships are built on things other than church.

My dogs.

My husband.

My self-care and recharging.

My patio on summer days.

It's not a bad thing to want to go home.

It stirs up gratitude that a place like this exists in my life, and the nomadic nature home takes on as I navigate different seasons of my life.

KONA + HER FLOWERS

I got a small German Short- Haired Pointer when I was in my mid-twenties.

She was given to me after a family could not keep her due to allergies and such.

I had NO idea what I was getting into.

I had roommates. I had like 4-5 jobs and I was away a lot of hours on weekends for work...yet I got a little crazy puppy.

I said, YES.

And gosh darn it, we grew up together. (Yes, I consider my 20's a time when I grew up).

She was there through friendships ending and beginning.

She moved into my apartment with me, living alone for the first time.

She helped me through boys, being afraid, and stressed me out by eating everything.

She made me love the dog park on Sunday mornings and the people who inhabit it.

She was there through meeting my spouse, getting engaged, married, and having our first kid. She started new seasons with us.

She raised our other pup.

She was central in my twenties.

She helped me grow up.

She made my house home.

She helped me understand the joy of ordinary moments in our days.

She left us last week. I held her close through the whole thing.

I made the call.

I still hope it was the right one.

I thanked her for being there for me, and for doing so well with what she was given.

Now our house is emptier and quieter.

We can leave the gates down, eat snacks, and leave food unattended on the countertops.

There is an ease that's already coming after that dynamic loss, helping me know it was right.

Something I wasn't expecting was the kindness of humans to surround this loss, making it sweeter.

A friend and coworker left flowers.

My parents gifted me a plant in her honor.

My SIL watched our daughter so we could be with Kona.

My besties left sunflowers and checked on us in the days to come. 30+ comments surrounding empathy, prayer, and love were posted on our social pages.

We saw those we love grieve with us.

We cried together.

We laughed together.

It reminded me of the goodness of people.

How much I need community, always. Especially in my pain.

It's reminded me to reach out when I'm soft and sad and cannot see straight.

It reminded me how interconnected we are with creation, how we sustain each other and make life richer.

That's exactly how Kona left her flowers.

Still guiding us along, waking us up with the wonder of being alive with others.

We will always love and miss you, Ko.

Thank you.

TO THE ONES WHO HELPED ME HEAL

When my world stopped turning, you sat with me while it did.

Instead of trying to get it to spin again, you simply said "Yeah, this is hard."

As I sorted through my pain, you were there on the angry days, numb days, and days that held unspeakable peace.

You were my advocates. My "yeah screw them" people.

You were also wise and patient, guiding me back to forgiveness.

You held my baby and held me. Offered advice and offered to listen.

These people held my hand as I evolved into who I am right now. They knew who I would be right here. They had the foresight.

And they sure as heck would not let me stop until we got here.

Healing knows no stranger or strange thing.

A book, a glass of wine.

A friend holding your baby.

My husband walking with me, no matter the mood.

My dogs in the sunlight.

Iced coffee in the sunshine.

My Christmas tree on December nights.

Resting instead of performing.

Trying new things, being a beginner again.

Watching spring return to my backyard.

Conversations with the ones who hurt me.

Walking into the building again.

Teaching about what I lost and what I love.

Finding my way back to church.

Friends having babies and birthdays.

My daughter turning one.

All of these were my guides and many many more.

God found me through every single one of these things.

He reminded me life is so full and gorgeous and hard and worth living.

I cannot thank him enough.

I cannot thank those people enough.

Thank God for the ones who helped me heal.

ABOUT ME RIGHT NOW

It's difficult to answer this question.

I'm intentionally trying to show up as my whole self in all areas of my life.

Work, marriage, parenting, friendships, family, and faith.

I'm better at that than I've ever been.

But that also leaves me vulnerable and exposed.

Wondering if I'm too much, if this thought is too liberal, or if I'm making _____ more complicated by overthinking.

I'm learning how to be a friend and receive friendship for what feels like the first time in my life. Good lord, my need to save and fix and be the one who is irreplaceable is next level.

I'm expressing my needs and preferences, even if they don't make sense or are not convenient for the other person.

I told my husband what I wanted for Mother's Day.

These are big steps for me. I combat the lie every day: they should just know. That equals true love in my mind.

IN WHAT WORLD IS THAT POSSIBLE?

There can be wins and intentions, but expecting friends and partners to be mind-readers is actually not love.

I'm allowing myself to see my body and perhaps stop viewing her with a skeptic's eyes. Maybe I can be proud of my post-breastfeeding boobs, my droopy tummy, and wide hips.

Maybe my growing wrinkles can be marks of life instead of worry lines.

I feel messy and confident.

I am riddled with guilt for yelling at my kid and working so much. I also love working and the independence.

My spiritual practices are allowing myself to do things just because AND denying myself every once in a while.

Being a walking contradiction is freeing right now.

UNLOCKED

To free from restraints or restrictions.

A LETTER FROM SUMMER CAMP

My character got assaulted today.

After I did some healing from a previous assault.

Same offender.

I'm tempted to let the healing wear off and sit right back down in anger.
It's justified.

I want everyone to know just how manipulative and ego-driven this leader is.

But what would burning down a town solve?

What rises in me when I am belittled and spoken down to?

Is it strength and grace?

This time, it was a smile—realizing insult and politics cannot touch me this time. I refuse to sink into the place of proving my worth and ability.

That isn't what the God I serve asks of me.

It isn't what my husband asks of me.

Nor my closest circle of friendships.

So, why would I do that for this leader?

This past week was not about proving myself or getting back into good graces.

I can truly say I was myself.

I led, I sang.

I was bold and quiet.

I was led, even though it was hard.

I cherished good relationships and conversations with folks I love.

I danced and sang my truth.

I drank way too much coffee and devoured many chicken strips.

I healed and remembered everyone's humanity.

I did not for a second do any of that for this man.

I did it for Jesus—or Jesus did it for me.

How unbelievably assuring it is to live freely, outside of proving worth.

I don't do it all the time, but this week I know I did.

And that is why I stand firm on the ground of who I've been created to be and what I will do.

As I write, I smirk.

I'm growing.

The opinions of others, even words of insult and assault...I'm learning to let it slide off of me. I exist in honey-like peace.

Heavy, warm, undiluted peace.

It's only from God.

It's only from His Spirit.

So, yes I did "learn and grow" and I did "do what was asked of me".

But it wasn't for you.

It was for me.

For my Jesus.

WHAT THE WILDFLOWERS SAY

A few months ago, as the weather turned chilly, I decided to go out for a run.

I was feeling a little risky and bored with my old route, so I took a new one.

I was feeling okay until my phone battery died and the road I'd mapped out didn't present an opportunity to circle back around.

So, what began as a two mile jog finished as a four and half mile panic-run as the sun began to set and it got darker and darker.

My heart was pounding out of its chest.

Survival mode came on...I just had. to. get. Home.

I withheld this specific panic attack for about half an hour until my husband came to find me. Once I got in the car, it released, and I sobbed.

So much bad could have happened, but it didn't.

I felt guilty for putting my spouse in a place of worry, thinking something had happened to me. But he only held me closer and kept whispering, "You're safe".

Fast forward to today.

I decided on a whim to re-run that route, armed with a full battery and location services. It was the day I would conquer my fear and overcome it.
To my wild surprise, as my feet hit the pavement of county roads, I found peace.

Don't get me wrong, there was sweat pouring from every place and my legs were tired. Running is never easy, don't believe anyone who tells you otherwise.

Anyway.

I had previously gone back to this panic-run route to map it out from the safety of my car, and to one day conquer it.

The turn I initially missed before now presented itself, and I took a right onto a road called Kline.

Our region is well known for its open skies and farmland and today's running views didn't disappoint. Along the pavement grew brush and weed before the corn or bean fields hit. I couldn't ignore the wildflowers this time around.

Bright purple, yellow, and orange.

Inviting butterflies and bumblebees alike.

As the summer sun beat down on my skin, I was guided gently to see that this run wasn't about conquering, but about listening and seeing the wildflowers.

Here is what they told me:

Lesson 1:
What's up with the word extraordinary? What's up with the quest to do extraordinary things? If I break down the word, it's EXTRA-ORDINARY.

Superbly usual.

You've done something EXTREMELY normal.

I laughed at all the times I tried to be extraordinary, and maybe even in the ways I am.

The more I am ordinary, the more I will learn to be extra-ordinary.

Lesson 2:

Just because you are found, it does not mean you will not get lost.

Or maybe I was never lost with God—He has always known me as "found".

Because of that, I feel ashamed when I lose him.

But part of the loss is so necessary.

I've lost a lot of God that has brought new hope to being found in Him.

As I made that turn, knowing I completed that part of my run, I stopped. The turn I initially missed led me to the most beautiful road, begging me to stop and take it in. I was found, but also still lost, not having run this road before.

Lesson 3:

I am becoming okay with my body. Learning the food patterns and reasons behind them. Understanding movement is not about being skinny; it's about being healthy.

It's not about laziness and giving up—I know what it feels like to sell myself short with goals and such.

It's more about understanding how food is connected to my memories.

My highs and lows.

So is exercise.

I read something once that begged women to give themselves a break on weight.

After all, the pizza that was eaten at 4 am was on a weekend was a time she felt most alive with those close to her.

The memories shared over food are what matters.

It may add 5 lbs, but who the heck says that's the end of the world?!

Bikini bodies are what we say they are, and a bikini looks good no matter where I find myself on the pendulum.

Lesson 4:
My social media and brand will be filled with humanity.
You won't find similar color themes or graphics—maybe you will, I don't know.
The common thread you will find: learning how to be human and finding God because of it.

Lesson 5:
I'm a gorgeous mess. And that's good. When I'm crying crazy (thanks, Lizzo).

Even when I'm waiting. Even when I feel lost.

It's not a pride thing, it's an ownership of all of me. Broken, faulty, talents, brains, beauty, insecurity, and grit.

I'm not broken. I'm whole.
And I'm human.

Lesson 6:
It's time to unpack.

The more I am ordinary, the more I will learn to be extra-ordinary.

I've had some suitcases packed in my current season, ready to run at a moment's notice. That sounds better than actually unpacking through hardship.

It's easier than digging my feet in and aligning with God and His church.

So, I have to unpack—while holding onto hope this season is not forever.

But it is my present, a gift if I choose to see it that way.

As I completed my quest, I not only conquered a fear but found myself in the wildflowers.

I look forward to the lessons they have to teach me in the future.

I AM

I'm too busy focusing on the reasons I'm not. I forget to remember the reasons *I am*.

I'm not skinny like her.

I'm not gentle or praised like her.

I'm not a good follower.

I don't have good boundaries.

I'm not I'm not I'm not.

If I'm not all these things, then what am I?

What am I left with?

I am a force.

I am funny.

I am dedicated to those I love. I am a contrarian.

I am a pastor.

I am a writer.

I am loving.

I am selfish and selfless.

I am a contradiction.

On the days I focus on my "nots", I need to remember how that feels.

The voice in my head is loud, emotions rule and experience does not.

I cannot trust myself or anyone else because they think I am when I'm set on being "not".

But today at 3:05 pm, I'll remember *I am.*

GETTING IT RIGHT

Maybe getting it "right" is just knowing my daughter is loved.

By God.

By us.

By her crew.

Maybe that's the foundation above all else.

Everything else will be built on this.

-God speaking to me about getting it "right" as a parent.

TAKE WHAT YOU NEED

Worth doesn't depend on productivity or lack thereof. It isn't built by the options of others. It stays, cultivated by the Careful Gardener.

Open your hands and receive the love and care you so freely give to others.

Allow yourself to be a beginner. There is wonder and strength in naiveté, you don't have to know it all.

God is proud of who you are. Beyond the work of your hands, mind, and heart–as you are. You are cherished.

Your life is supposed to look different than others. It's time to release the small-boxed life the comparison mindset forces you into.

You carry it all so beautifully with grit and grace. You can set it down. You can ask for help. You are your world's helper, not savior.

God is never tired of you.

God always welcomes us–prodigal and proud. The Kingdom table has room for both.

Consider joy instead of criticism.

Yes, there is a lot in front of you. But you have what you need within.
Strength for today, bright hope for tomorrow.

There is no right way to grieve. No brownie points for healing first. Allow the setbacks, the joy, and the complexity.

Be gentle with yourself, friend.

I'M NOT NICE

I got a sticker yesterday that said "Nicest person ever."

Guys, it was a sticker and I'm still thinking about it. I laughed and joked with co-workers about how I actually don't consider myself to be nice...

But when others agreed with me, my laughter turned nervous. My face got hot. My eyes welled up with tears.

"Oh, they agree with me...", I thought. "Oh."

So, I'm spending some time today with the weird baggage a simple sticker brought up. I've always wanted to be a really sweet/nice person.

But I was created with some fire I sometimes wish I didn't have.

I have a face that speaks before I do (good or bad).

I feel complex.

Most days I can own that and live freely in it. But today it feels a little harder to do so.

I want to be kinder, and not jump to conclusions.

Choosing to encourage instead of degrading someone I disagree with.

I want to just listen and be able to not question when ppl tell me what to do.

My point?

Maybe I'm just reminded to see people.

Maybe I should think twice and not laugh and agree when someone degrades themselves—even (sometimes especially) if they're joking.

And maybe I'm saying it's okay to be sad about parts of yourself.

It's good to see yourself honestly and hold space for that person.

And maybe I'm saying let's do better by letting ourselves and others be human. Super complex and beautiful—all wanting to know we belong.

ABOUT ME RIGHT NOW

I feel like a layer has been peeled back in my life.

Or a contact has been put in so my blurry vision can become clearer.

I have been given the gift of presence and perspective, seeing my life as truly INSANE and beautiful.

What God has given me, where He has placed me...so intentional.

And I usually just ask for the next thing or deem it not "good enough" based on crap metrics that don't make sense.

I remember writing words while I was a worship leader that I now use as lectures.

I didn't know what they were for when I wrote them. I just hoped the season of waiting would be over soon and I could be free.

I remember feeling empty and sad that the season working with a team had ended. Now, I'm a part of a team that I feel at home in.

I remember wanting to make a difference in the church, lead a program, wanting to be trusted to build something...and here I am, doing just that.

Ridiculous trust. Space to grow and make mistakes.

We live in a house now that has closed out the first chapter of our marriage and work in ministry. It signifies a new season we're building together.

It looks different, but it's so good.

I'm ready to get back to work with my contacts in.

Settled and curious.

BIG GIRL BEDS AND JESUS

I put my daughter to bed in her big girl bed tonight.

No prompts, just kept a routine and she jumped right in.

A few weeks ago, she put her leg over her crib. Freaked me out, so here we are.

I'm so proud.

I'm so sad.

Being a parent is feeling the fiercest highs and the darkest lows...my whole body responds to my daughter and the emotions she calls out of me simply by being herself.

I'm dumbfounded and swollen with pride that she's sleeping right now.

And I'm reminded of a few things I tend to forget.

God isn't the helicopter parent. He's a trusting God that provides the next steps for us.

And what is a big deal to God sometimes just feels like living to us.

I wonder if God swells with pride when we do big kingdom things we don't even comprehend. And perhaps God is raising us to be independent while also remembering we can always run back home.

My faith holds both.

The tender mom-heart and the deep pride and awe of someone so little, yet so fierce.

Life is a wonder.

WHAT DOES IT MEAN TO SHOW UP AS MYSELF RIGHT NOW?

1. Gentle with thoughts about my body.

2. Gentle with my lack of motivation and apathy towards ALL things.

3. What if I trusted people when they say they value me instead of feeling the need/responsibility to keep it that way?

4. Bringing my whole self to the table...the cranky, sparkly, and soft bits.

5. Doing work that has boundaries. Doing good work.

6. Acknowledging burnout. Holding space for my sadness, fear, and loneliness with the Church. With faith. With Christianity.

7. Allowing the "long-game" mentality. In my marriage, parenting, work, my body.

DOWNTOWN

I'm sitting in the sun after my therapy session. The breeze is welcome after an hour of crying and hard work. I hope this is in a book one day.

Therapy notes on my iPhone...maybe I'll call it that.

Today I felt like God was proud of the work I was doing. That it honored him.

Who I am honors him...and I haven't felt that in a while.

Therapy brings awareness to the boxes around me...how I've been existing within them.

Shrinking to belong.

I don't know how to not shrink to belong quite yet, but I'm working on it.

And I'm going to start trusting the people in my life who want me to bust out of these boxes just as badly as I do.

Being Christlike is not simply a submissive stance.

It requires megaphones, foot washing, diaper changing, shattering glass ceilings, going to therapy, and creative warm environments...there's room for ALL of it.

There's room for you.

There's room for me.

Not just room, but FIELDS of possibility.

I'm working on believing that, too.

MAYBE

Maybe I can be the one that feels the sun on their skin.

Maybe I can be the one who shows up for my daughter and her body without shame.

Maybe I can be the one who signs up for a 6 am spin and sleeps in when she needs it.

Maybe I can be the one who builds a program and says no.

Maybe I can be the mom my daughter needs me to be.

Maybe I can be the one who trusts her body.

Maybe I can be the one to trust myself.

Maybe I can trust others want to help and show me love.

Maybe I can receive and enjoy friendship without performing and controlling.

Maybe I can enjoy the good without guilt.

Maybe I can encounter the hard without thinking I've done something to deserve it.

Maybe I can trust that my husband cares about what I need, too. Maybe.

THE YEAR THAT SHALL NOT BE NAMED

2020 certainly has brought us some lessons, right?

Now we find ourselves halfway through and we've endured a pandemic together. Our eyes have been ripped open to the racial injustice that still exists.

We feel messy and messed with.

We've also endured social media throughout this time. Holding it as a gift in one hand and a grenade in the other.

Some claim it's the end times as they watch the news. Some hold tighter to party lines as a new election looms. I've seen us choose each other and fight each other.

My oh my, how this year has exposed us.

Our privileges.

Our prejudice.

Our idols and priorities.

Our true opinions on each other...on those who disagree with us. We've been shoved outside of what we know.

We're not living in normalcy anymore.

We are awake and afraid; clinging to any kind of security and control we can find.

So, where is God?

Some have said he's cleansing our nation, calling it to repent. Others have claimed God is testing us.

Some say He's punishing us.

Some say He's renewing and redeeming.

I'm not sure I have an answer.

Maybe it's all of the above.

I've learned not to be so quick to assign a reason or purpose to seasons I don't understand.

I do believe this: God is waking us up to the injustices that grieve his heart.

God has restored what is important to Him in our 40-day shelter at home.

His love for us is beyond what we can do.

The gift of family and togetherness He gives us.

He showed us how much we need each other.

He showed us we are not in control.

He showed us we are not god.

He showed us how celebrating each other lifts the clouds of harder seasons.

He showed us the power of prayer.

He has stripped us, leaving our hearts raw.

All of this and more.

> *I've learned not to be so quick to assign a reason or purpose to seasons I don't understand.*

I truly believe because our hearts are raw and because we have learned so much about loving each other, we are now more receptive to His voice.

We're quicker to listen and respond.

And as we're being asked to speak out and advocate for our brothers and sisters of color, we again are being presented with a choice.

Do we cling to control and what we know, or do we surrender to once again not knowing?

Quarantine has shown us that God moves in weird ways.

Maybe He's asking us to trust He's moving us once again towards true unity and freedom.

For ALL of us.

If God's heart is for redemption, I'd say we choose to trust Him.

THE SOAPBOX

So, since you're here...

I think we miss something when we say, "Jesus died because all lives matter".

I wonder if we're called to listen with open hands and hearts to those who feel their lives don't matter.

Maybe we're called to show how much they matter, though history has shown them they were nothing more than a people to be looked down upon. A people to be enslaved.

Jesus did that on the regular—with the Samaritan woman, with the prodigal son.

His new law included Gentiles, the outcasts of society (you and me, fyi).

It was hard for some to accept another group of people could inherit God's blessings. Why? Because it made His love and law vast and wide for more to know Him. That means we all get to be a part. No elitism. No above-ness.

Heck, this is the purpose of the cross.

Yes, he laid down his life for all to know they matter.

But in doing so, He also afforded us the chance to say that your specific life matters without taking the worth away from my life.

Aren't we called to lift up the weary, poor, and oppressed?

The voiceless and downtrodden?

Right now, a majority of us are not in those categories.

This doesn't mean we don't have pain or hard times, that unifies all of us.

"This is my command: love one another the way I loved you. This is the very best way to love. Put your life on the line for your friends."

Look outside yourself, my friends.

Look into the heart of God, and read how He values the life that feels lifeless in your bible.

Acknowledging and joining arms with our brothers and sisters of color is something in this world that will pass into eternity.

Statues, flags, and country pride will not.

Political leanings will not.

Heaven on earth, this is our call.

Do you hear it?

WEIRD REMINDERS AND PERMISSION SLIPS

It's okay to unfollow people and accounts. It's not forever. I learned from a friend recently that if you need space,are triggered, or just not helped by someone/thing in the online world...you can take the space you need.

You're worthy of that.

It's okay to build a life that doesn't make sense to other people, friends, followers, or even your family. I've been in the habit of shrinking myself in various ways my entire life to gain approval or permission. Turns out, approval or permission isn't given the way you want it to be or from who you desire it.

It's something that can be found within. From your Source, not from anyone else.

It's okay to not text back right away. Take the space you need.

Letting yourself feel the pain is not the same as finding the reason for the pain. In therapy recently, I was explaining to my therapist all the reasons I could feel triggered by a scenario I was working through, giving reasons for responses. She gently reminded me to stop existing only in my head without feeling it in my heart and my body. This means I have to sit with the pain and feel it in my body. Feel it all again. Let myself be triggered and vulnerable...it's a way harder route. But I have seen this is the right and holiest route.

Find friends who hype you up. Friends who know that returning to lead worship for one random Sunday is a big deal. Who come to your speaking events with coffee and presence. Who show the heck up for life, holding bad days and good. Who cheer on your marriage, love your spouse, and kids so much. These friendships are worth holding out for. Worth trusting people again.

Worth it. Hands down.

Book vacations or little weekends away--find your joys in the winter in the Midwest. It's a holy practice to look forward to things AND sitting and waiting for spring to come.

You can think differently and still have a seat and voice at the table.

It's SO hard to be a beginner at things as you get older, be it a hobby or career. But I think this is what it means to build a life you love and are proud of. When I step back at the things my daughter will find out about my life, it makes me smile. Learning to snowboard at 32. Building a program after heartbreak. Jumping into a life in creative ministry. Holding my boundaries. How her dad and I fell in love and continue to love our life together. Releasing a book. It's all so hard. And it's so worth it.

Stick with outfits that feel like you.

Take a look in the mirror every once in a while and remember how much life has happened and yet, here you are.

Wiser with more creases around your eyes and smile.

A heartier laugh and life more glorious than you could have ever imagined or hoped for.

A WORD ON COMPARING PAIN AND EXHAUSTION

I had a student stop by my office this week. As she was listing her pain and feelings, she stopped herself and proceeded to say, "But I know my profs have families and legit reasons to be tired."

"The reasons I'm tired don't feel like enough."

I'd like this to stop.

It really bothers me when parents with kids under 5 say to people without kids, "OH YOU THINK YOU ARE TIRED?!"

Like anyone who doesn't have kids or hasn't experienced *their* personal version of tired doesn't get to be the MOST tired. The MOST TIRED award only goes to them.

What about the college student staying up until 4 am with stressors like deadlines, friendships, spiritual growth, tensions, etc.?

What about the single guy in his 30's who struggles with insomnia and depression?

What about the mom who spends the whole day worrying if their son will be shot at school or on the way home?

Everything I listed is exhausting.

And everyone is living with their version of it.

It's ironic and hilarious and sad to me how we try to win the exhaustion game.

We make our weariness a race! You need to be doing XYZ to be able to complain about being tired. You can't be tired if you're not doing anything!

Not true.

A different and kinder narrative is to stop comparing our weariness. We don't value ourselves or our life's seasons when we say this.

I was exhausted in high school, college, post-grad and working 5 jobs, working in ministry, being a mom...I was tired regardless of the season. I am tired regardless of the season.

Why?

Because life is tiring! Our bodies are not meant to carry it all, full tilt, all the time. We need to set things down. Just for a bit or maybe indefinitely.

So, here's my white flag in the exhaustion race.

I'm not running it anymore.

I'm not going to assume I'm more tired than others.

I'm just carrying a different load.

It's a small shift and maybe it won't have tangible results.

But it will help someone feel less judged and pressured when you say, "Oh man, that sounds tiring" instead of "Oh man, you have no reason to be tired!"...and other terrible responses of the sort.

We need softness and comfort more than ever.

ABOUT ME RIGHT NOW (FINAL EDITION)

I'm at Starbucks on a Friday morning. It's been a hard and emotionally exhausting week. I've also been struck with how grateful I am to have a spouse and kid that feel like home.

I like salads for lunch. More than sandwiches and big meals. It gets attention from people–it feels shame-y. I'm over it. It's good for me and the energy I need for my day.

This week I've felt like a hypocrite a lot. I post words that are celebrated and struggle to live them out the next day. I don't know how to live up to the high standards I have for myself.

I feel anxiety when I rest multiple nights in a row outside of the weekend.

If I'm not meeting with people or producing, I feel shame and fear. I'm working on it and running from it...interested to see how this lesson shakes out.

I am noticing how lifting heavy weights is shaping my body and I like it.

And this feels different than past obsessive gym stages. I move for more reasons than just being smaller.

I move because it helps the cloudy and oppressive thoughts lift.

I move because it's an investment in my kid and my spouse.

I move because I want to hike in my 80's, I want to run with my kid's kids (if she so chooses).

I move because I like how it makes me feel.

I move because I believe in the balance of eating what you love and honoring this body given to me.

I move because I want my daughter to see a relationship with health and fitness that is a work in progress.

I move because some days piss me off and I want to shake it out.

The long game...health and wellness. Whole-heartedness. Trusting my body with all of it. It's a hard journey with so many outside pressures and expectations...but taking it back for myself has been sweet.

I have a LOT of feelings about this work I've put together over the past 10+ years of my life.

Big feelings about releasing my personal journals of pain, tension, waiting, joy, and work into the world. Opening it up for judgment, comparison, and literally everything else.

Yet, vulnerability always breeds community, trust, and solidarity.

So, I'm thinking it's worth it.

This is an exercise in trusting my voice and trusting I have things to say.

Trusting I'm worthy of being loved and heard, regardless.

And so are you.

ABOUT YOU RIGHT NOW

A word for you.

I'm not sure how this book found you.

Boxed up.

Broken down.

Bruised.

Building. Belonging.

Whatever era you find yourself in, my challenge and prayer for you is to *grow* through it as you go through it.

Lean into those hard feelings.

Lift your eyes every once and awhile.

Feel the warmth of the sun on your cheeks and skin.

Notice the trees dancing in the wind as the seasons change.

Tell your friends the hard stuff.

Be honest with your partner.

Kiss your pet and watch trash tv.

Live against the normal rushed pace.

Take the time you need to heal.

Eat good bread and bake on Sunday afternoons.

Live a life people don't fully understand.

Post goodness on the internet.

Embrace your life as it is.

Talk about what you're learning.

Talk about what's hurting you.

Talk about opportunities and gifts given to you.

It's all meant to be shared before the big red bow is tied up. Life is not meant to be boxed up and presented.

It's meant to be opened up and shared.

Consider trying this.

It's a choice.

It's the hard road, undoubtedly.

It's also the way that brings life more meaning than we have words for.

Holding joy, pain, devastation, new life, and ordinary-boring days–
it's all a part of it.

Thank you for letting me share my last 7 years with you.

ACKNOWLEDGEMENTS

To Joel: I'm so glad we got married and are building such a gorgeous life together. Thank you for believing in me and my voice so much and pushing my dreams forward with me. This would not have happened without you as my cheerleader and advocate. I love you.

To Ari: You have cracked me open in ways I never thought possible. You are our greatest gift and the love of our lives.

To Kona: Thank you for being the best pup and growing up with me.

To Kem: Thank you for seeing me through this work and using all the tools in your belt to help this project go into the world. More so, thank you for being my friend.

To Valerie: Thank you for seeing your story in mine and for bringing your careful eye and convictions to this work.

To Emmi: The unique and original avatars you created are more than I could ask or even dream of. The original creative direction you brought through the is brilliant and I'm grateful to have a piece of you in this book.

To Gene, Brenda, Kristin, Jess, Liv, Terry, Mark, and Joel--thank you for giving your time to digest this work. For all the wisdom and encouragement. Doing spelling and grammar checks while cheering me on. Your time, words, and support mean so much through this process.

To my launch crew: Thank you for giving me the kindest and most wonderful boost. For helping me find the courage to step out and take up space.

To my community, family, and crew--you know who you are. Thank you for carrying me and walking close through it all.

A FINAL NOTE

As I comb through this work at this point in the publishing process, I'm tempted to edit and clarify. To clean things up and put bows around learnings.

Months and years have passed since this work has been written. Seasons experienced have closed, busted open, and been revisited with clarity again and again through the publishing process.

It's like catching up with a good friend you haven't seen in years.

It's tempting to talk about the shiny parts and good things only. To give the short version of a longer story. To present yourself in the present, not the past.

If we sat down to catch up over a cup of coffee today, I'd do my best to share my life with you. The good parts, the hard parts, and all the ordinary parts in-between.

I'll do my best to keep a pace that backs all the talking I've done in these pages.

I honor who I was when all this was written. What I knew. What I didn't. And I honor all of the stuff to come.

I pray you will find the freedom to the same.

EDITORS + CONTRIBUTORS:

Joel Graves, Olivia Alexander, Kem Meyer, Valerie Schuett, Emmi Meyer, Jess Lyons, Kristin Baker, Terry Linhart, Mark Waltz , Gene Troyer, Brenda Troyer.

ABOUT THE AUTHOR

Becki currently resides in South Bend, IN.

She holds her Masters of Ministry from Bethel University. Her work background consists of creative and worship ministry, teaching and directing programs in higher education, and mentorship. Currently, she works as the Director of Worship Arts at Bethel University (IN), leading and teaching within the program.

She is the oddball who loves work meetings and weeknight plans. In her free time, you can find her trying new cookie recipes, using voice-to-text to spill her thoughts on the notes app, and sipping her iced americano (with an extra shot).

More from Becki here:

www.beckijeangraves.com

Made in the USA
Monee, IL
30 January 2024

51965468R00108